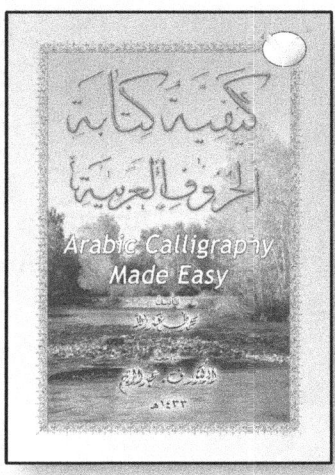

كيفية كتابة
الحروف العربية

Arabic Calligraphy
Made Easy

تأليف
عفيف بهنسي

الشركة العالمية

هـ١٤٣٣

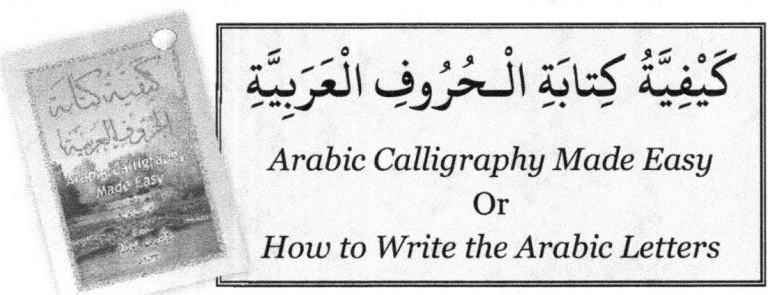

كَيْفِيَّةُ كِتابَةِ الْـحُرُوفِ الْعَرَبِيَّةِ

Arabic Calligraphy Made Easy
Or
How to Write the Arabic Letters

Copyright © 2012 by Peter Wood Young (a.k.a. Muhammed Taha Abdullah)

TAHA ARABIC BOOKS (KT 0294726-K)

ISBN : 978-967-0428-07-9

Second Printing

Please visit both Dr V. Abdur Rahim's website for the Arabic Language, and particularly mine for additional material and tips relating to calligraphy, the Arabic Language, teaching methodology as well as a complete teacher's guide (كِتابُ الْمُعَـلِّم) for the seven-book children's series :

www.DrVaniya.com   **www.Taha-Arabic.com**

Shukran! شُكْرًا! Thank you!

مَعْلُوماتُ الدَّارِسِ/الدَّارِسَةِ

آسْمُ التِّلْمِيذِ/التِّلْمِيذَةِ : _____

الْعُنْوانُ : _____

_____

_____

_____

آسْمُ الْمَدْرَسَةِ : _____

آسْمُ الْأُسْتاذِ/الْأُسْتاذَةِ : _____

الْفَصْلُ : _____

السَّنَةُ : _____

رَقْمُ الْهاتِفِ : _____

مَعْلُوماتٌ أُخَرُ شَخْصِيَّةٌ

_____

_____

_____

_____

Table of Contents

◆   ◆   ◆

● Part One / الْقِسْمُ الأَوَّلُ :

The Letters in Their Isolated Forms / الْحُرُوْفُ مُنْفَرِدَةً

◆   ◆   ◆

● Part Two / الْقِسْمُ الثَّانِي :

The Letters in Their Connected Forms / الْحُرُوْفُ مُتَّصِلَةً

◆ ◆ ◆

● Part Three / الْقِسْمُ الثَّالِثُ :

الْحُرُوفُ الصَّعْبُ خَطُّها / Difficult Letters

◆ ◆ ◆

● Part Four / الْقِسْمُ الرَّابِعُ :

Various Exercises : Written and Oral / تَمارِينُ مُخْتَلِفَةٌ : تَحْرِيرِيَّةٌ وَشَفَوِيَّةٌ

● ● ●

● ●

●

Flipping pages 11-40 produces a 'mini-movie' in which you can see the letters being drawn, step-by-step.

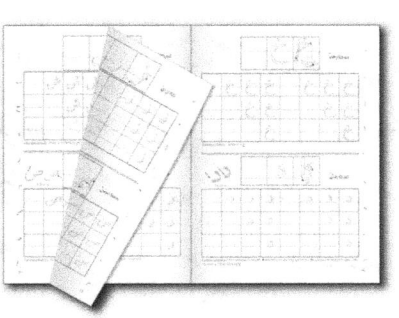

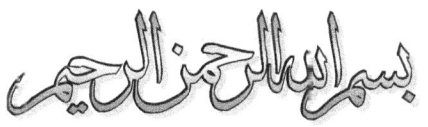

الْمُقَدِّمَة / PREFACE

This book is a hands-on approach to basic Arabic calligraphy. It is meant to be used, and used practically. It contains ample space for practice, and is very suitable for the classroom. It was originally designed for adults who wish to learn practically and independent of a teacher, then I modified it to be more suitable for children.

This book deals with the most basic of fonts, **Traditional Arabic**, which I've found to be the most common computer font, as well as the easiest font to read and write for beginners.[1] As you probably know, even though having someone teach is always favorable, you will benefit more in either case by understanding and following these subsequent points :

1. There are 29 letters in the Arabic alphabet. Of these, there are 18 shapes. Note these examples :

The letters in these two groups have the same *shape*, differing only in their *dots*. (See pages 9 and 10)

2. In general, letters have four *forms* : Initial, medial, final and isolated forms. Note these :

      Initial   medial   final   isolated

3. Although Arabic is written right-to-left, some of the letters may start left-to-right! (Like this). So, before you actually start, just look at the letter you're about to write—as silly as it sounds. Stare! (Did you do it?!) Really. Simply appreciate the way you are about to write the letter.

4. Pay attention to the arrows and dotted lines as they not only show where to start, but also show the proper angle which is needed for the letter to be written with respect to itself, and with respect to the 'ground line' as well as any 'side' lines.

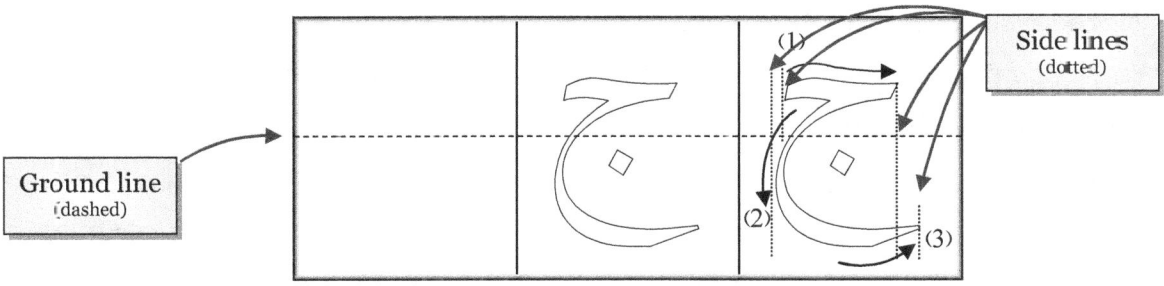

---

[1] Note the difference in these fonts (shown in regular and **bold**) which are popular in modern Arabic programs :

- Traditional Arabic : إنّ الخطَّ جميلٌ. إنّ الخطَّ جميلٌ.
- Simplified Arabic : إنّ الخطَّ جميلٌ. إنّ الخطَّ جميلٌ.
- Rekaa : إنّ الخطَّ جميلٌ. إنّ الخطَّ جميلٌ.
- Akhbar MT : إنّ الخطَّ جميلٌ. إنّ الخطَّ جميلٌ.

5. Be aware of the common mistakes in the 'Incorrect' sections.

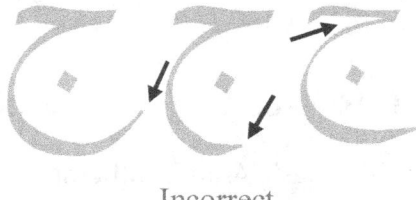

Incorrect

6. For best possible results, use a broad-tipped calligraphy pen as shown below. However, any chisel-shaped, wide pen (or marker) will serve your purpose just fine. Or, make it yourself!

 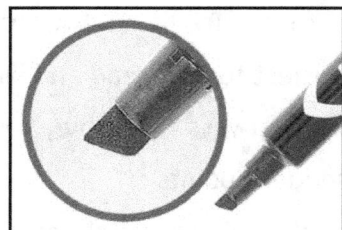 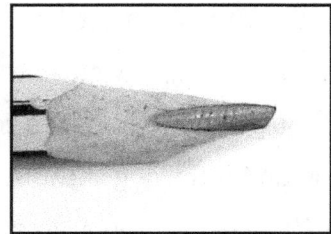

7. Page 9 shows the 18 fundamental *shapes* of the Arabic letters. Page 10 shows the same but in *outline* form. Although not necessary for this book's exercises, a simple (and inexpensive) way you can achieve this outline form is by using two pencils taped together like this :

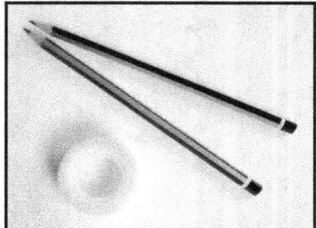 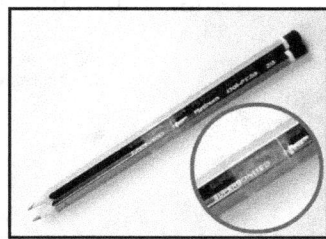 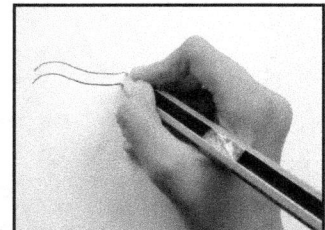

8. In the first section of the book; **Part One** : *The letters in their isolated forms* (pgs. 11-26) there are two letters per page. Do **not** complete writing all the lines of each letter. Instead, begin with the tracing of **only** the two outlined letters (as seen in # 4), as you get a feel for the letter. Then, in the third blank space, try it yourself. Go to the smaller version of the same letter on its following line, and complete the drawing of **only that one line**. After this, continue on to the *next* letter and repeat these steps. When you have completed this section and all the letters in it, repeat it. However, this time do the *second* line of each letter noting the mistakes you may have made during the first writing. After completing the entire section and all the letters this second time, write the letter in the *third* line for the final time. **Repetition is essential**. Doing this is better than writing each letter on all three lines all at one time, and repeating any mistakes made, over and over again.

9. Upon the finishing of the first section, continue to the second part of the book, **Part Two** : *The letters in their connected forms* (pgs. 27-38) with the same procedure mentioned above. Please keep in mind once again, despite Arabic being a right-to-left writing system, not all letters can be connected from the left. *(This is a bit similar to cursive writing whose rules can be quite tricky.)*

10. From there, continue on to the third section, **Part Three** : *Difficult letters* (pgs. 39-44). I've put this flower sign ✤ next to the letters which are included in this category throughout the book.

11. Finish the book by completing the fourth section, **Part Four** : *Various Exercises : Written and Oral* (pgs. 47-50). The words in this section have been made even smaller, and it combines all the previous rules, as well as introduces vowel points not previously mentioned. The empty spaces are for oral exercises. Start with (1) isolated letters, and then move on to (2) connected letter combinations.

12. Only simple letter combinations are mentioned. Those such as مـ خـ جـ هـ have been avoided.

13. Flipping pages 11-40 produces a 'mini-movie' in which you can see the letters being written. These are for the 18 shapes of Arabic letters previously mentioned, and not all the Arabic letters.

14. There are additional materials at : ***www.Taha-Arabic.com*** (Children's Book, First Level)

Special thanks goes to brother Raja Afiq Aizzuddin bin Raja Ahmad for his keen checking that not only did the letters meet from all (or most) possible angles,[1] *but also to ensure that the letters were written in correspondence with the rules based on traditional Arabic books of calligraphy.*[2]

Dr V. Abdur Rahim's many personal comments are also thanked.

──────────────────

[1] For example, the letters : ل and ح and د can be joined as follows : لحد as well as : لحد, but not all fonts allow both ways.

[2] This is important as fonts can connect letters in ways that may not conform to the rules. Note these examples :

- The letters : س and ر should traditionally be connected with the last 'lip' of the letter س raised slightly.

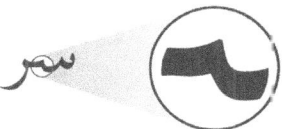

However, most fonts do not allow this, and so it becomes written like this :

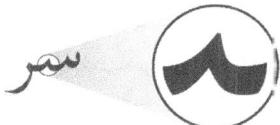

- The letters : ث and ن and ي —for example—should be connected like this (ثني). However, many fonts do not allow this and so it becomes written like this : (ثني). [Nevertheless, Dr V. Abdur Rahim mentioned to me that choosing 'non-ligature' mode during the set-up process of the program solves this problem. This may, however, only apply to older programs.]

- The letter ي (or ى) should be connected immediately to the letter before it like this (في). Programs—due to the 'justification' function—allow for the stretching of these two letters so they may become (فـي). The same is for (إلـى), and (لـي), and (نبـيّ) etc. So, the more proper way of combining these letters is as follows : (في),(إلى),(لي), and (نبيّ).

- The bottom 'lip' of the letter (ص) should *not* be written in it's final form. (i.e. : when it is *not* connected from the left). In Traditional Arabic, however, it appears in *all* situations. Take note of this example in comparison with the Mus-haf (i.e. the written Qur'an)

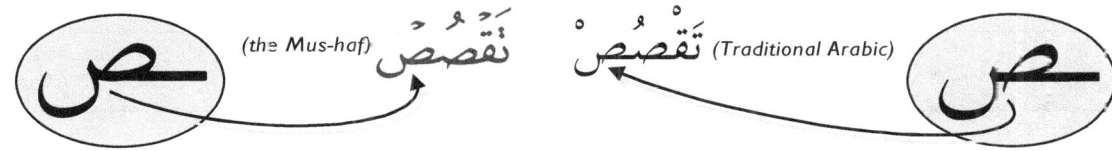

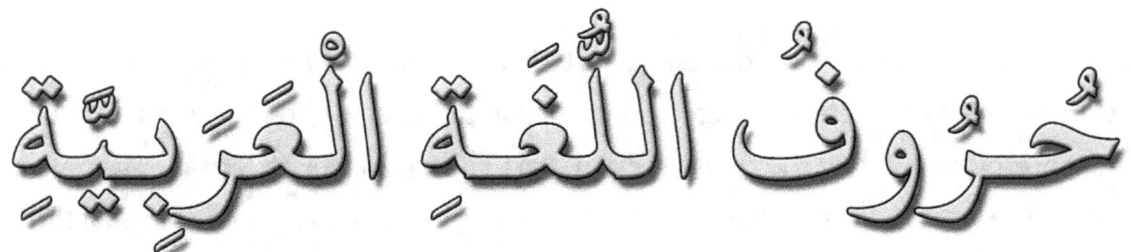

The Arabic Alphabet (all forms)

ح	ج	ث	ت	ب	ا
ح ح ح ح	ج ج ج ج	ث ث ث ث	ت ت ت ت	ب ب ب ب	ا ا

س	ز	ر	ذ	د	خ
س س س س	ز ز	ر ر	ذ ذ	د د	خ خ خ خ

ع	ظ	ط	ض	ص	ش
ع ع ع	ظ ظ ظ ظ	ط ط ط ط	ض ض ض ض	ص ص ص ص	ش ش ش ش

م	ل	ك	ق	ف	غ
م م م م	ل ل ل ل	ك ك ك ك	ق ق ق ق	ف ف ف ف	غ غ غ غ

ي	ء	و	ه	ن
ي ي ي ي	أ إئ ؤ أ ئ	و و	ه ه ه ه	ن ن ن ن

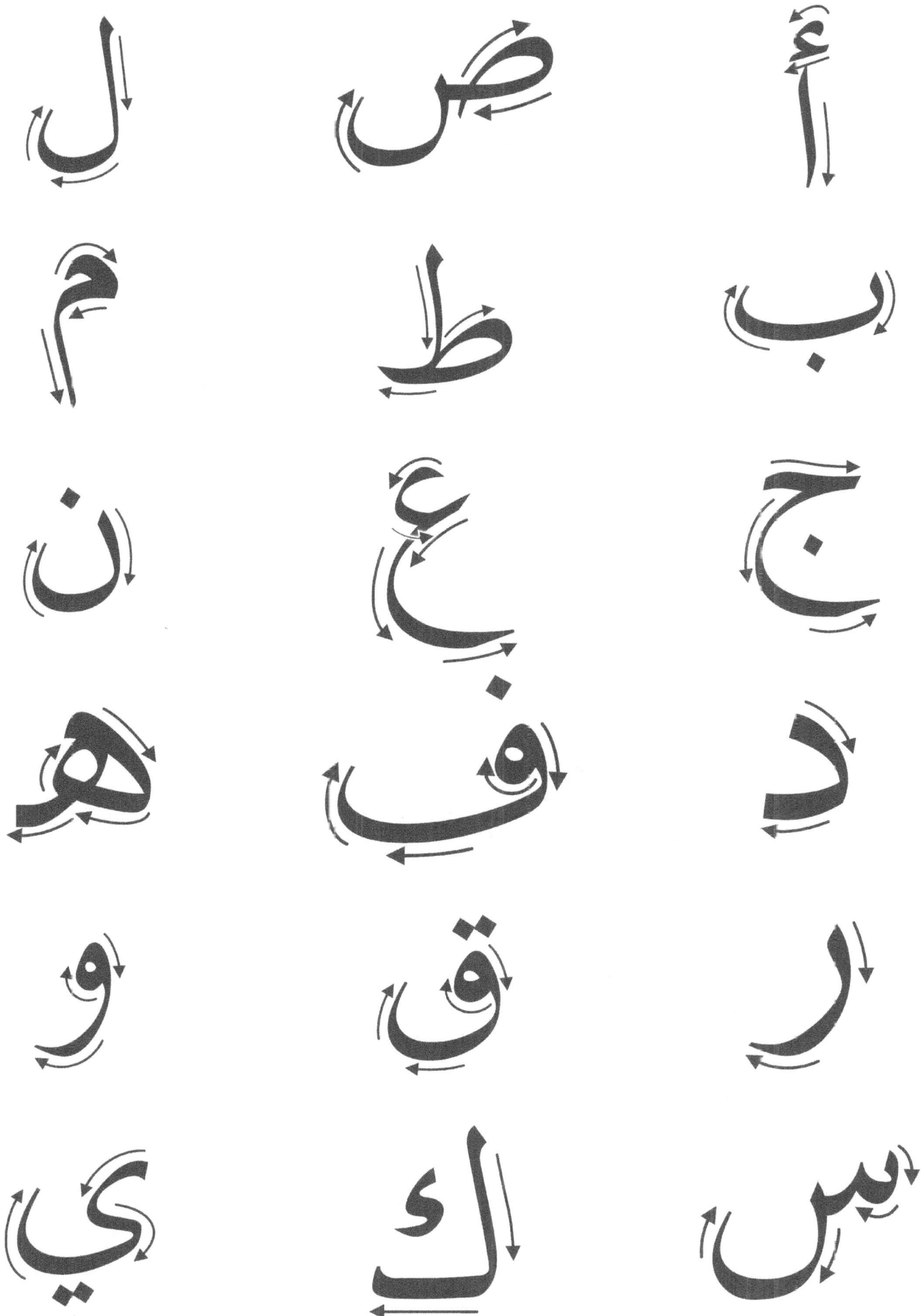

9

The Fundamental Arabic Letter shapes (Outline)

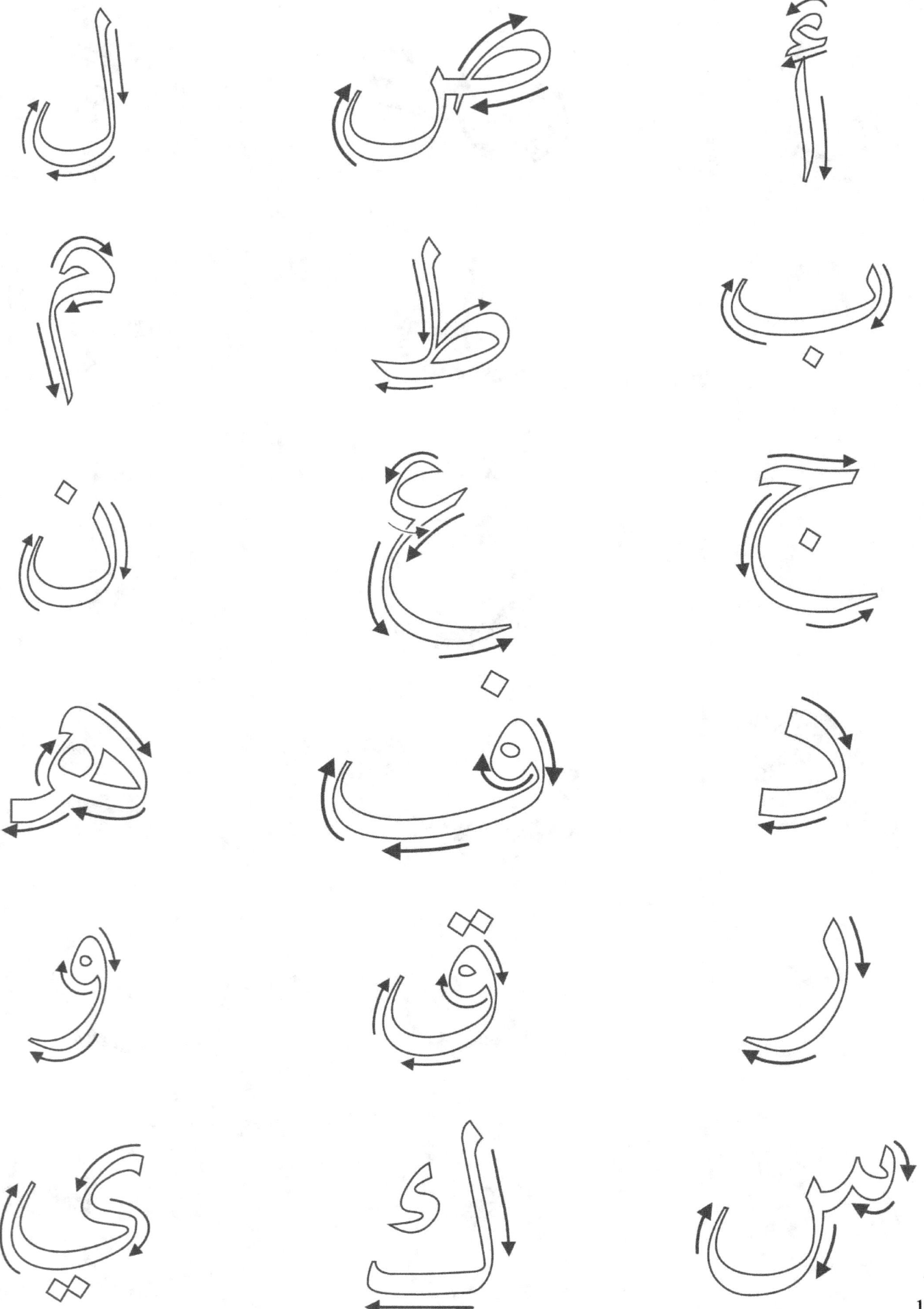

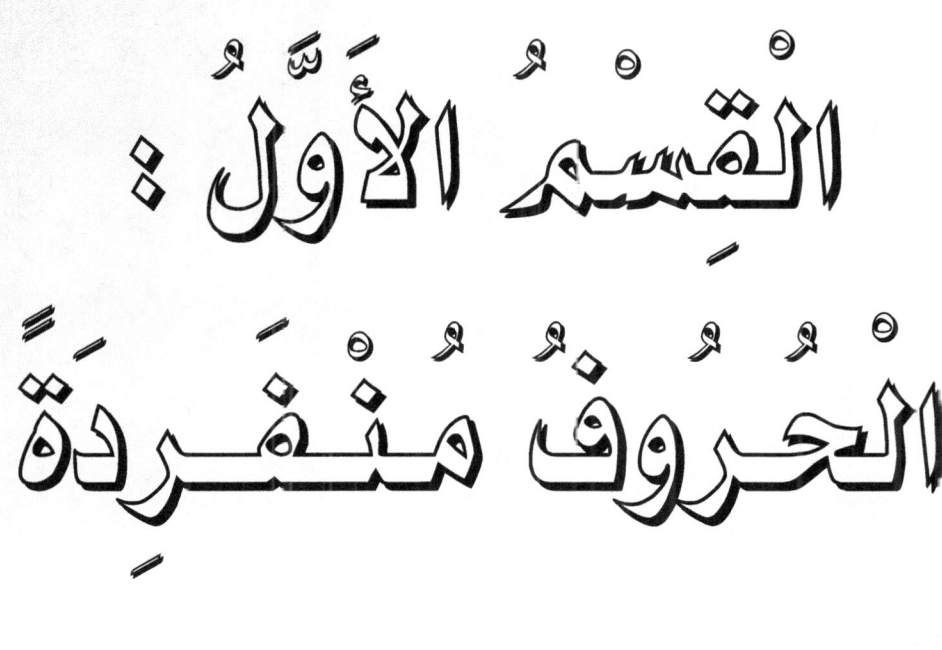

الْقِسْمُ الْأَوَّلُ :

الْحُرُوفُ مُنْفَرِدَةً

Part One :

The Letters in Their Isolated Forms

Incorrect

أ

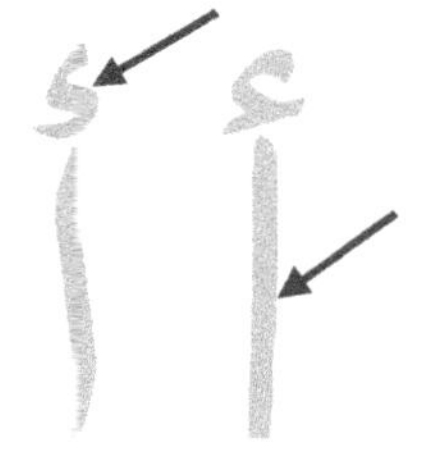

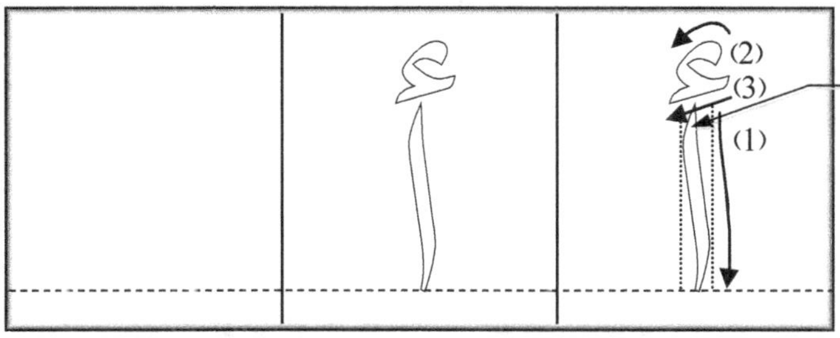

Begin here drawing *inside* the sketch using the lines as a guide as well as the 'mini-movie' (pgs. 11-40)

أَلِفٌ مَعَ هَمْزَةٍ

Alif with Hamza*

ب

ج

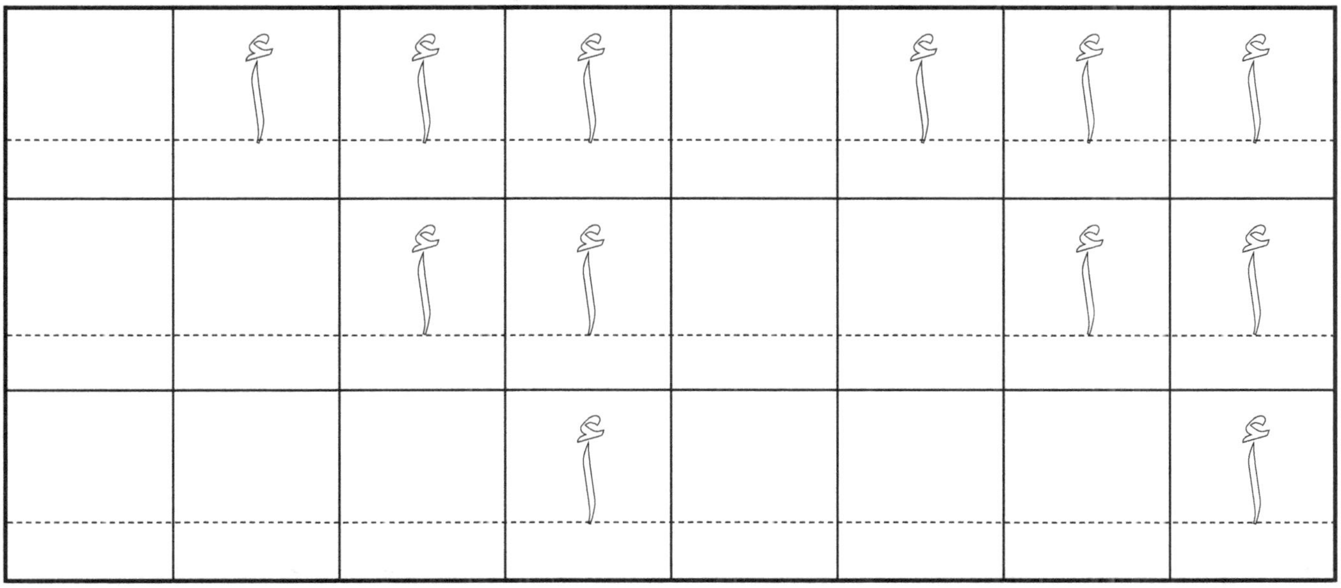

د

Common mistakes : *Drawing the Alif (ا) too straight. The Alif should be slightly curved and angled as indicated by the arrow in (1).* ● *Drawing the Hamzah similar to the inside of ك. These two differ [ء ك].* [Note : Incorrect]

ر

Incorrect

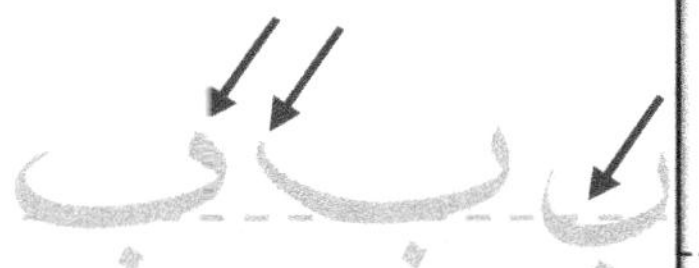

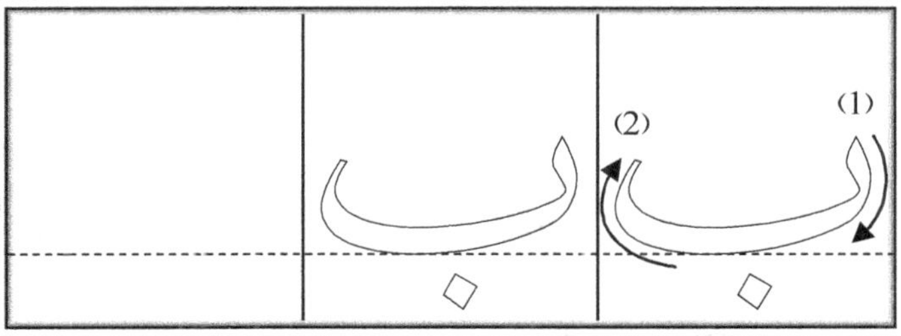

بَاء/Baa

س

ص

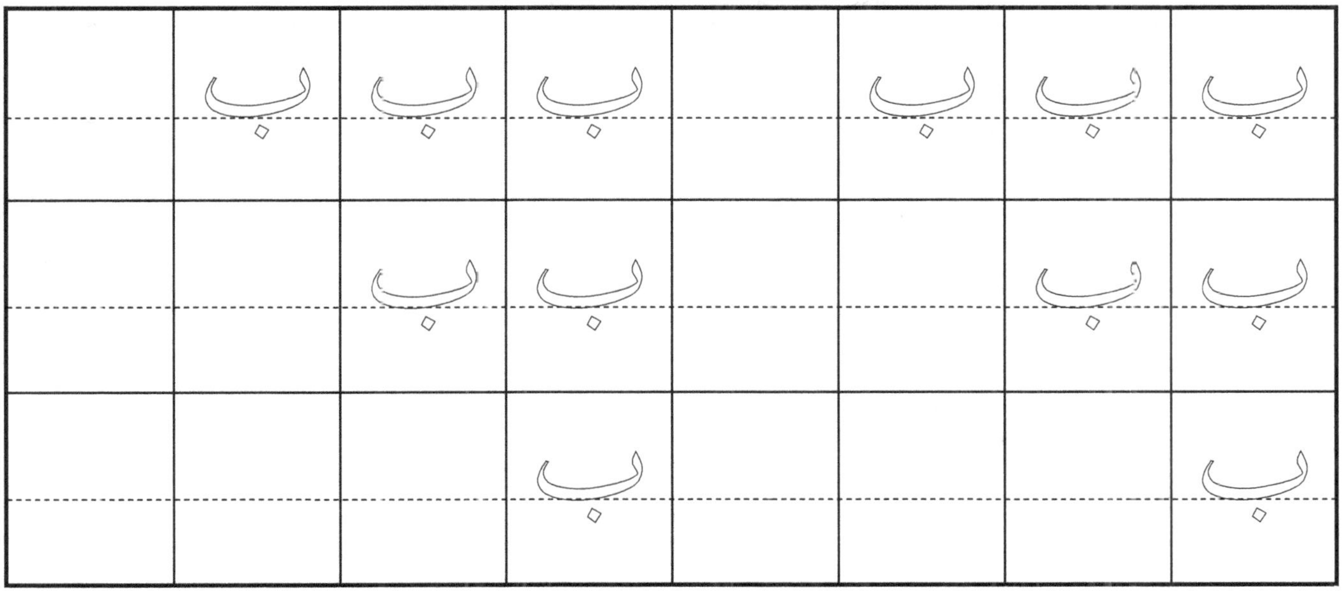

ط

Common mistakes : *Not curving the Baa (ب) backwards slightly as in (2).* ● *Drawing the letter below the ground line.* [Note : Incorrect]

ع

* Please note that these are actually *two* letters; (ء) written on top of (ا).

13

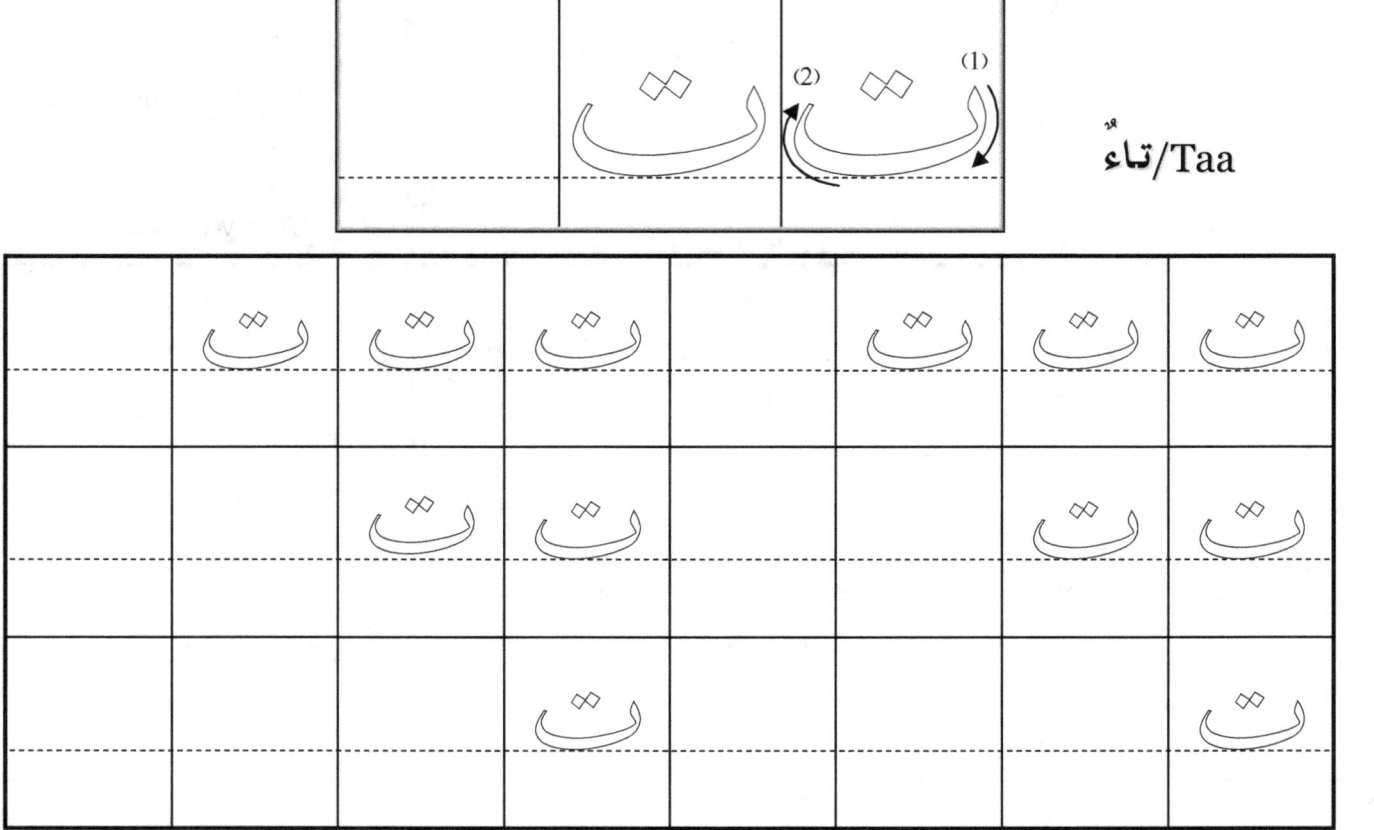

تاء/Taa

Common mistakes : Same as in ب.

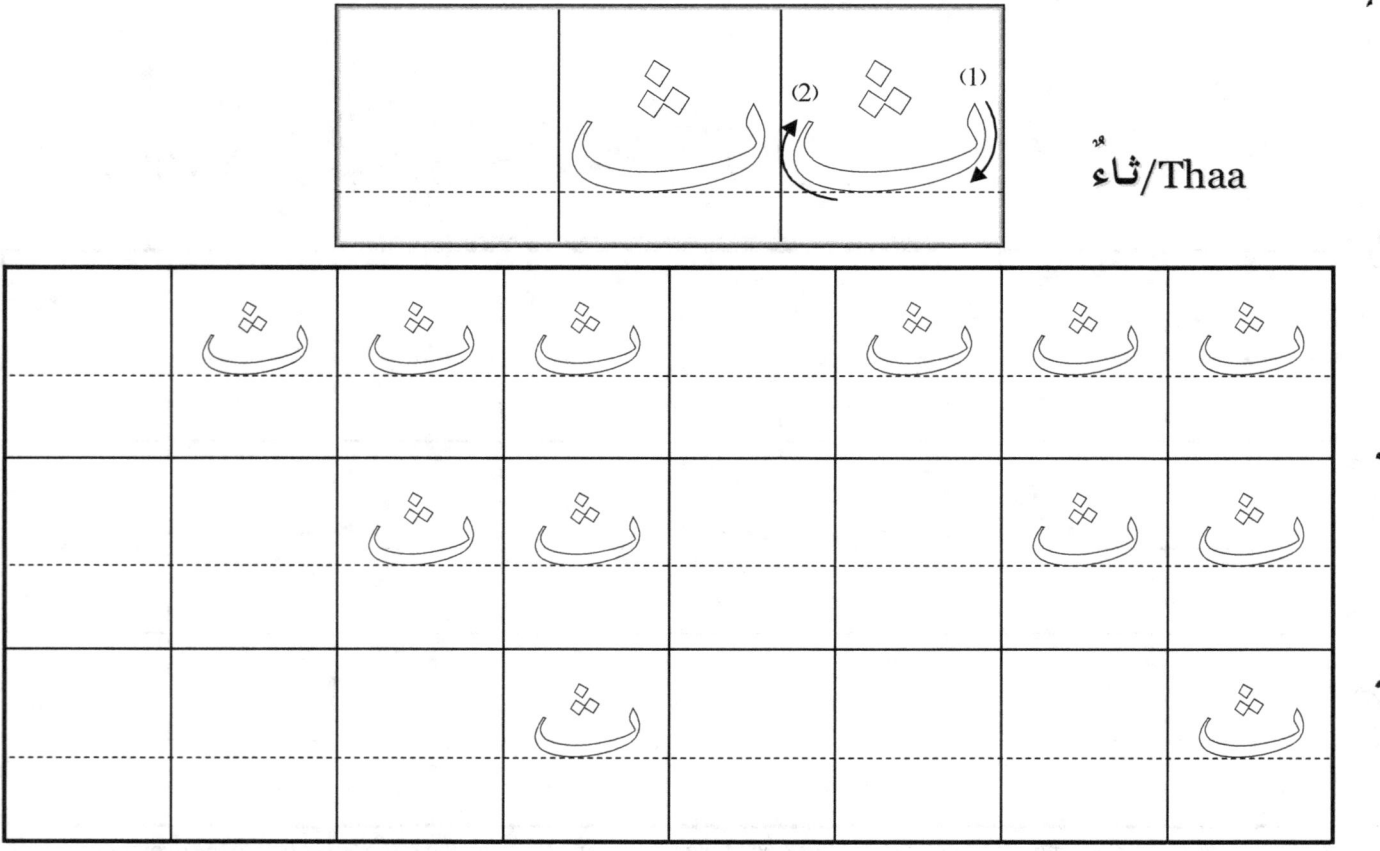

ثاء/Thaa

Common mistakes : Same as in ب.

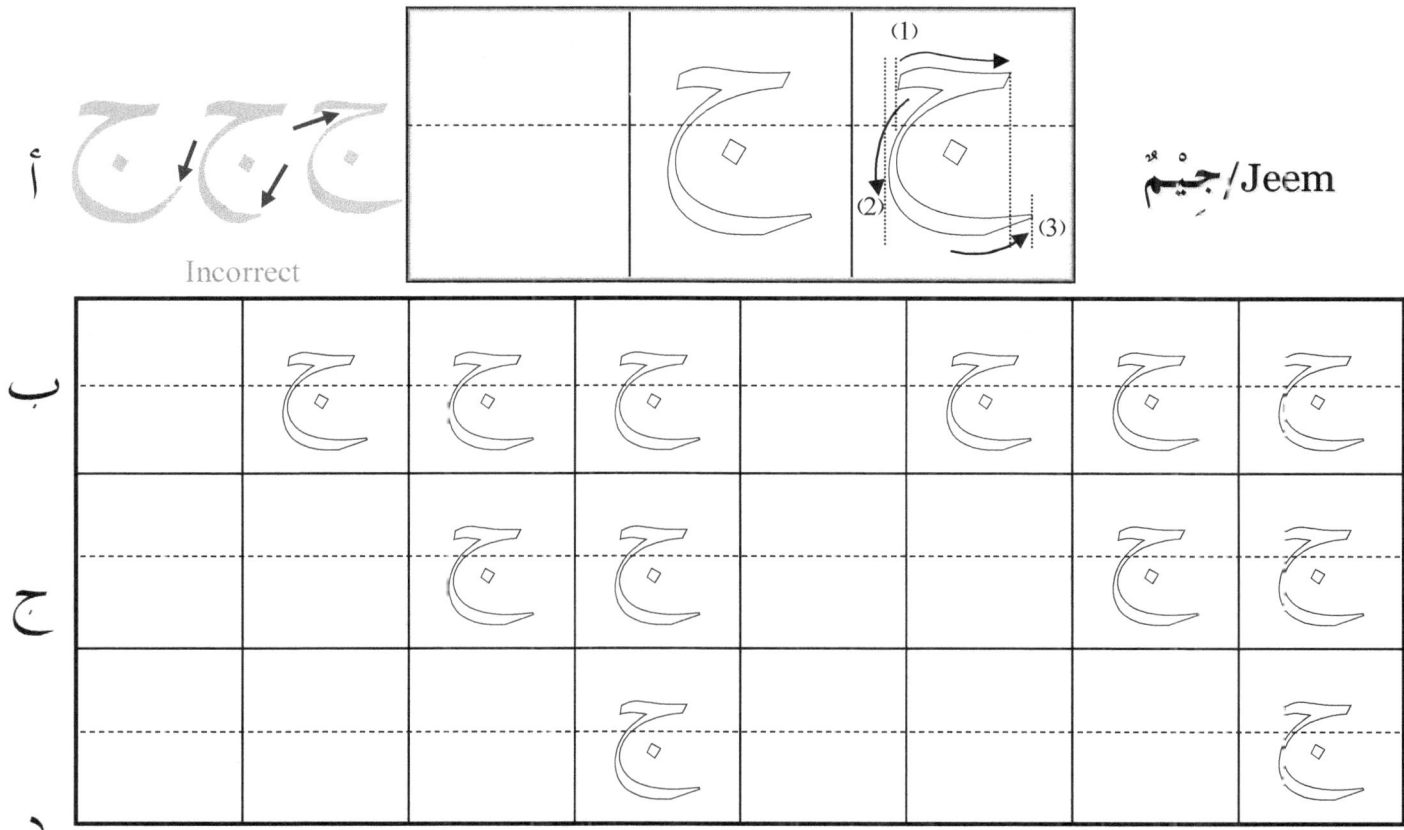

جِيْمٌ/Jeem

Incorrect

ا

ب

ج

د

Common mistakes : *Drawing (2) without retracing backwards from (1). [Note : Incorrect]* • *Not extending (3) enough.* • *Extending the drawing of (3) too far to the right, or too high.*

ر

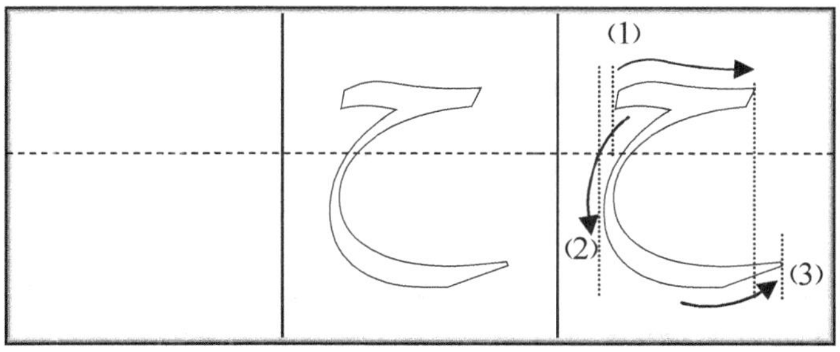

ز

حاءٌ/Haa

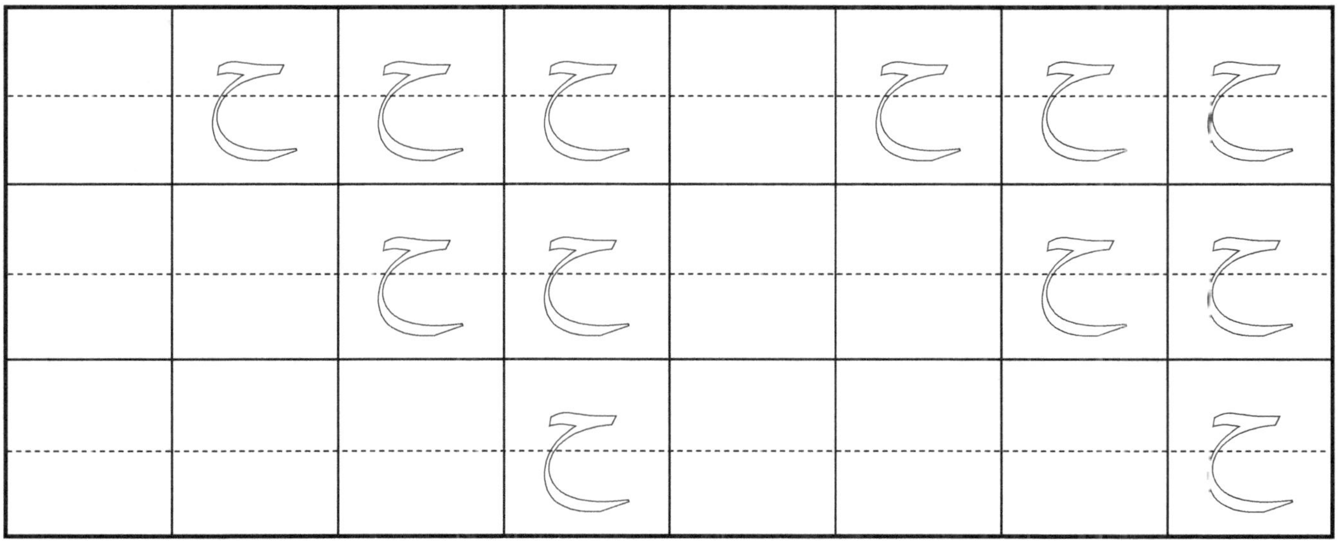

ص

ط

ع

Common mistakes : Same as in ج .

15

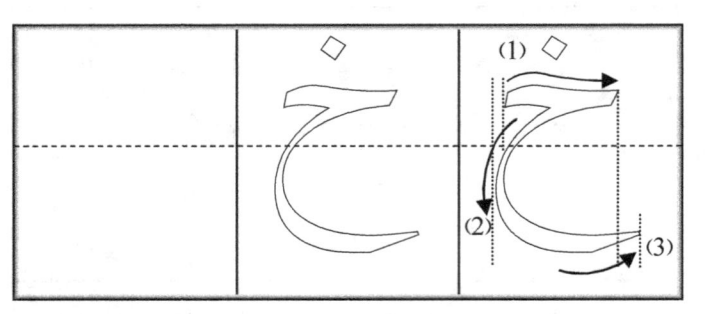

خاءُ/Khaa

Common mistakes : Same as in ج .

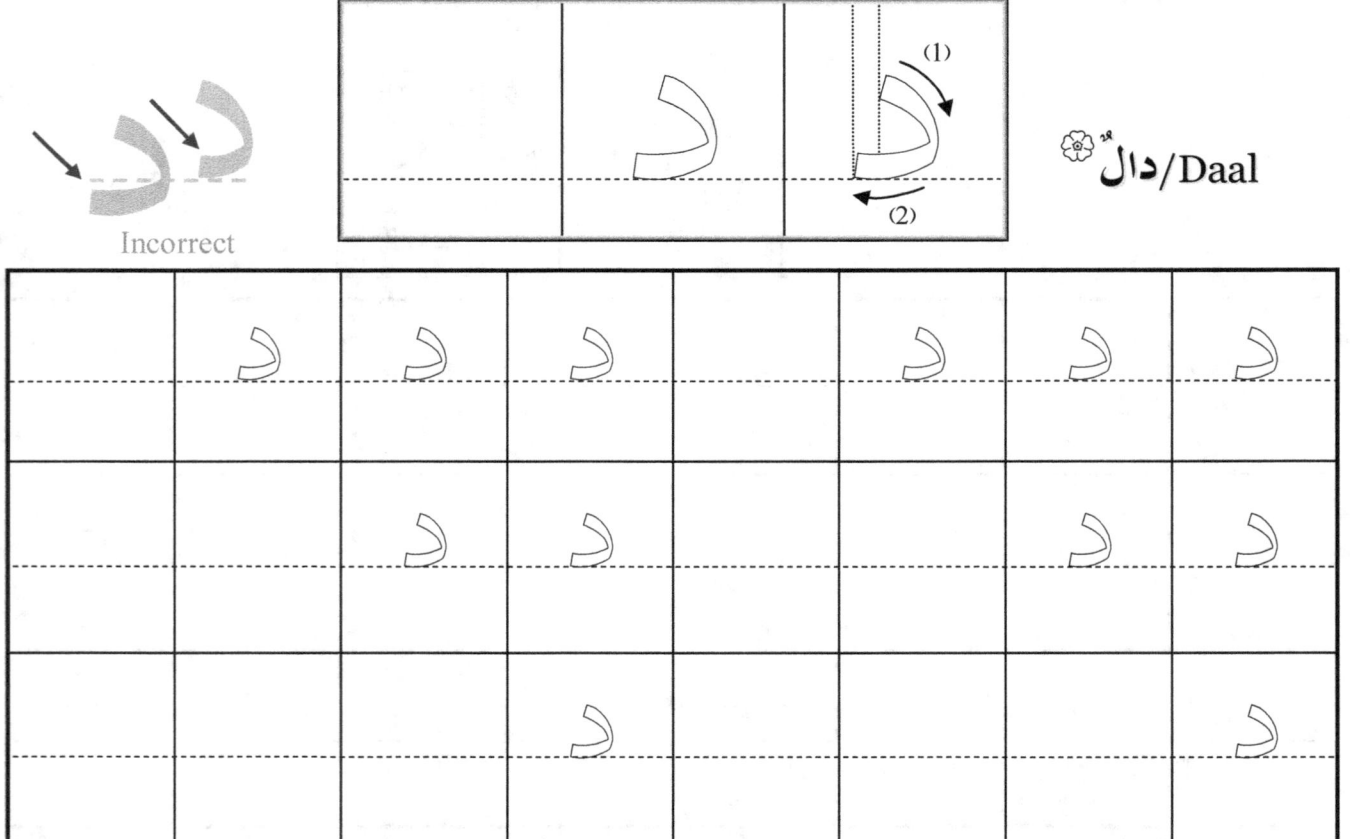

Incorrect

دالُ/Daal

Common mistakes : Not extending (2) enough. ● Extending the drawing of (2) below the ground line making it appear like the letter ر . [Note : Incorrect]

16

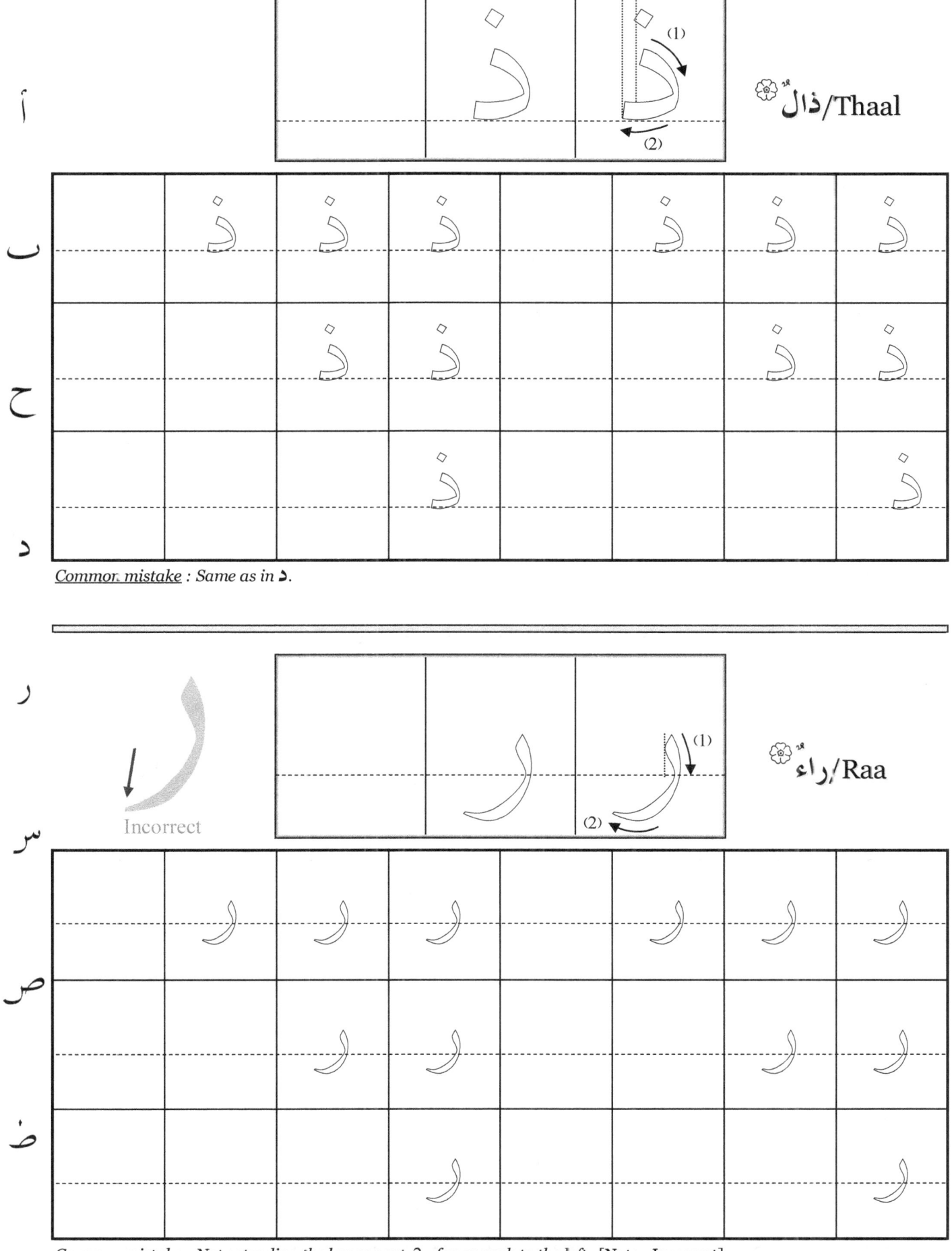

ذالٌ/Thaal

Common mistake : Same as in د.

ر/Raa

Incorrect

Common mistake : Not extending the lower part (2) far enough to the left. [Note : Incorrect]

أ

ل

ح

د

ر

س

ص

ط

ع

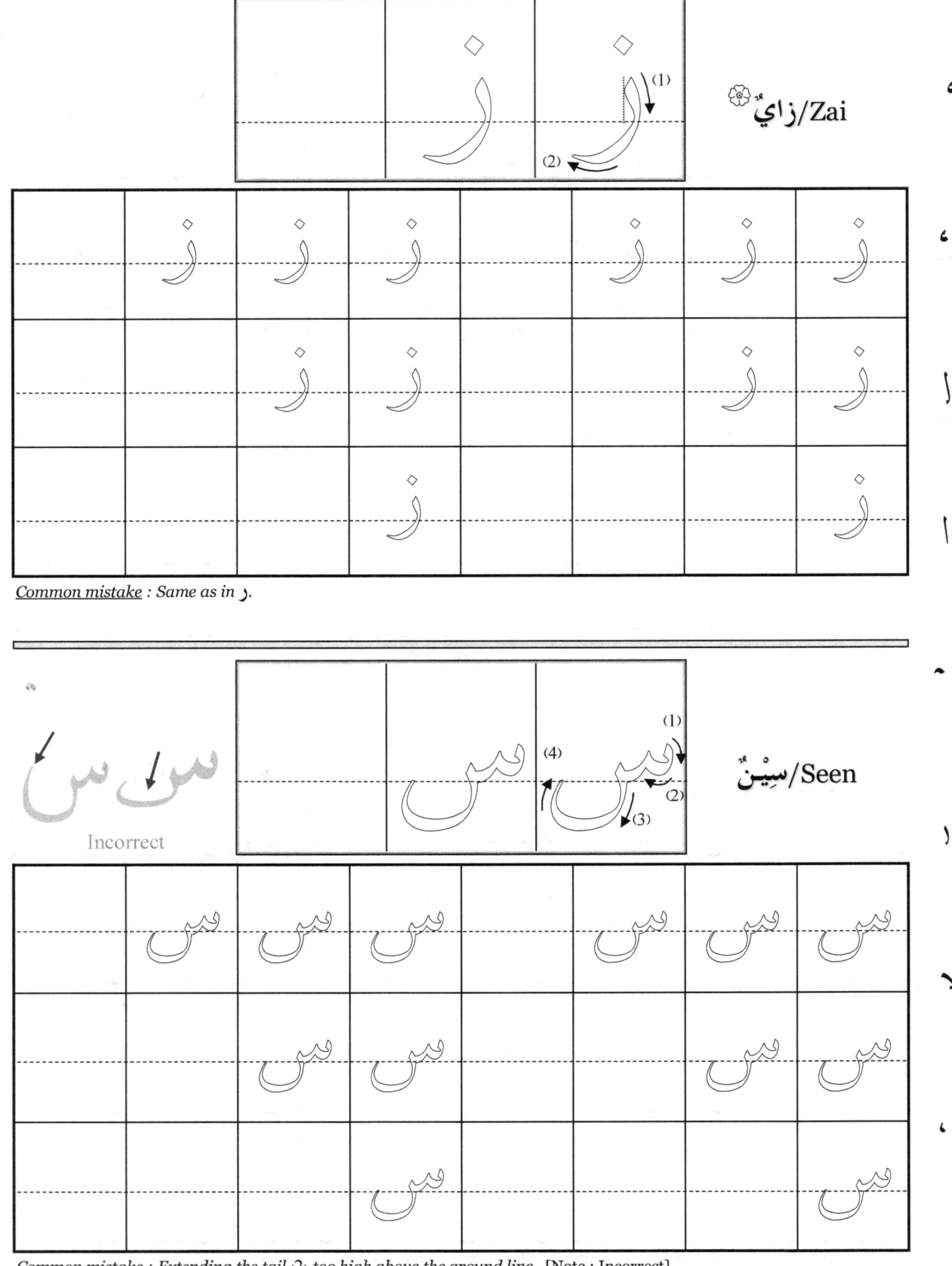

زاي/Zai

Common mistake : Same as in ر.

سِينْ/Seen

Incorrect

Common mistake : Extending the tail (2) too high above the ground line. [Note : Incorrect]

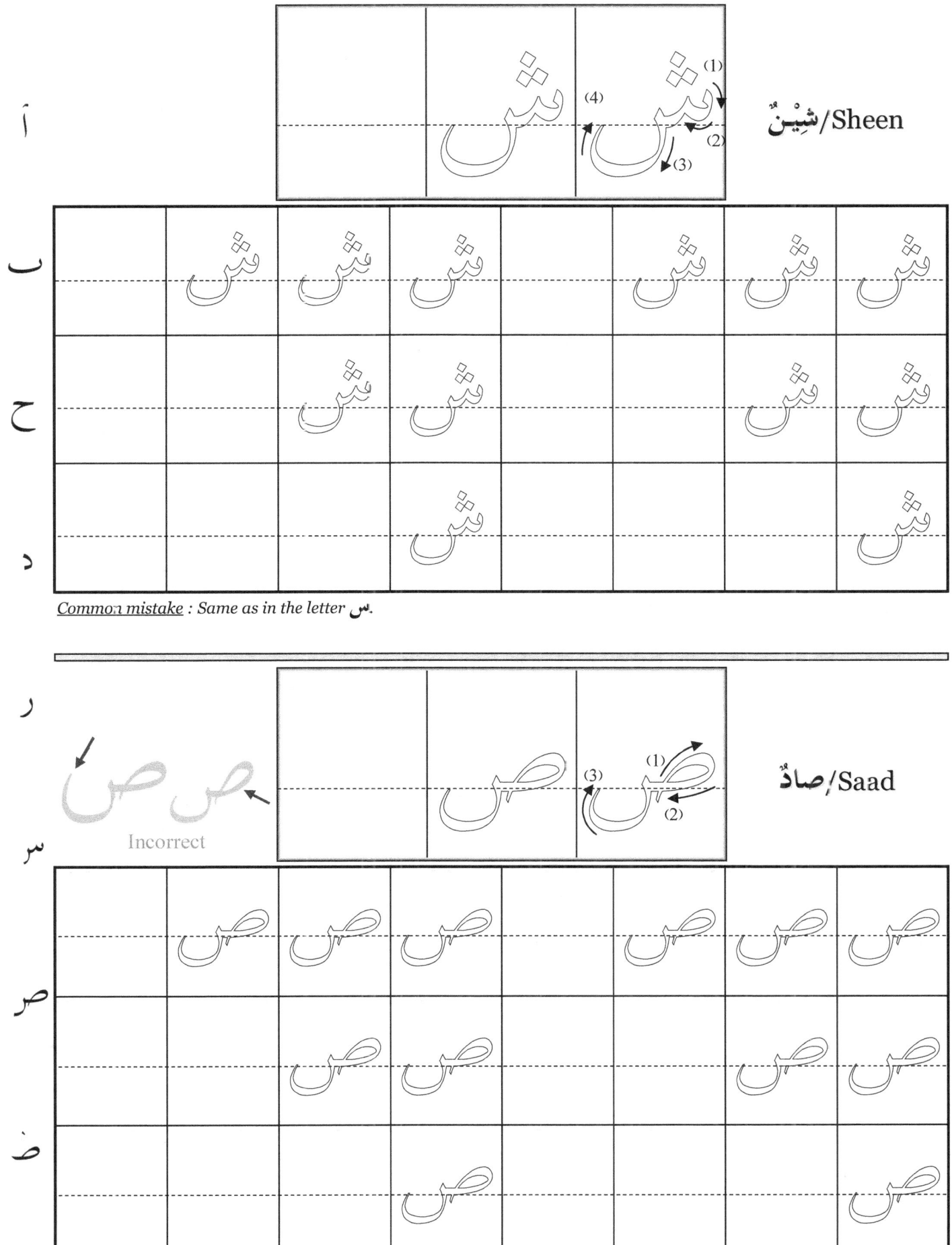

ا

ب

ح

د

شِيْنٌ/Sheen

Common mistake : Same as in the letter س.

ر

۳

صاد/Saad

Incorrect

ص

ض

Common mistakes : Not returning to the ground line as in (2). ● Extending the tail (3) too high. [Note : Incorrect]

ع

19

ه ‏ضادٌ/Dhaad

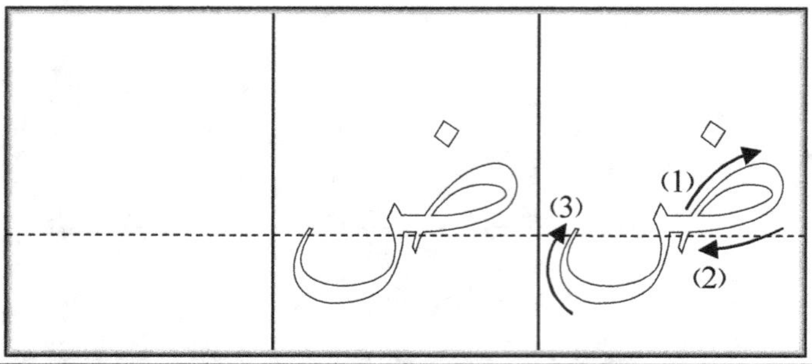

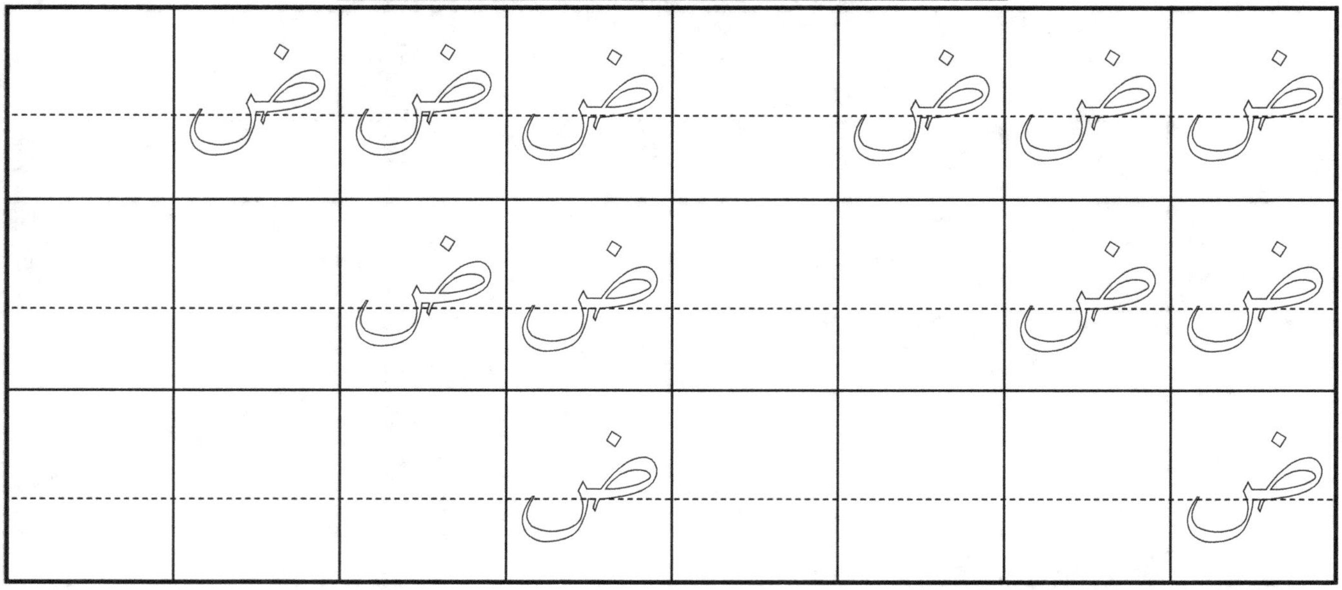

Common mistakes : *Same as in the letter ص.*

ظاءٌ/Thaa

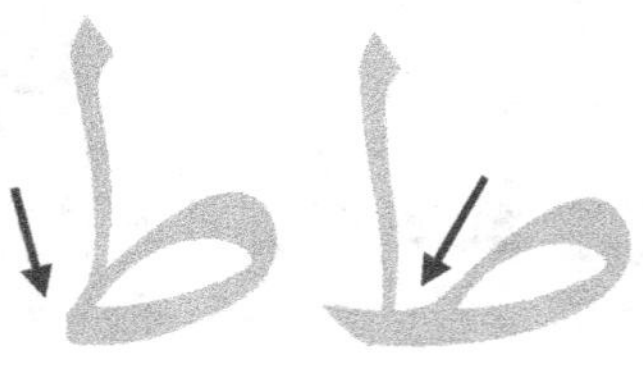

Incorrect

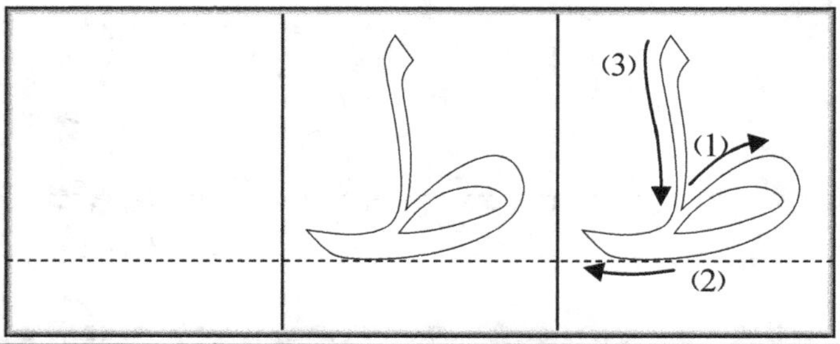

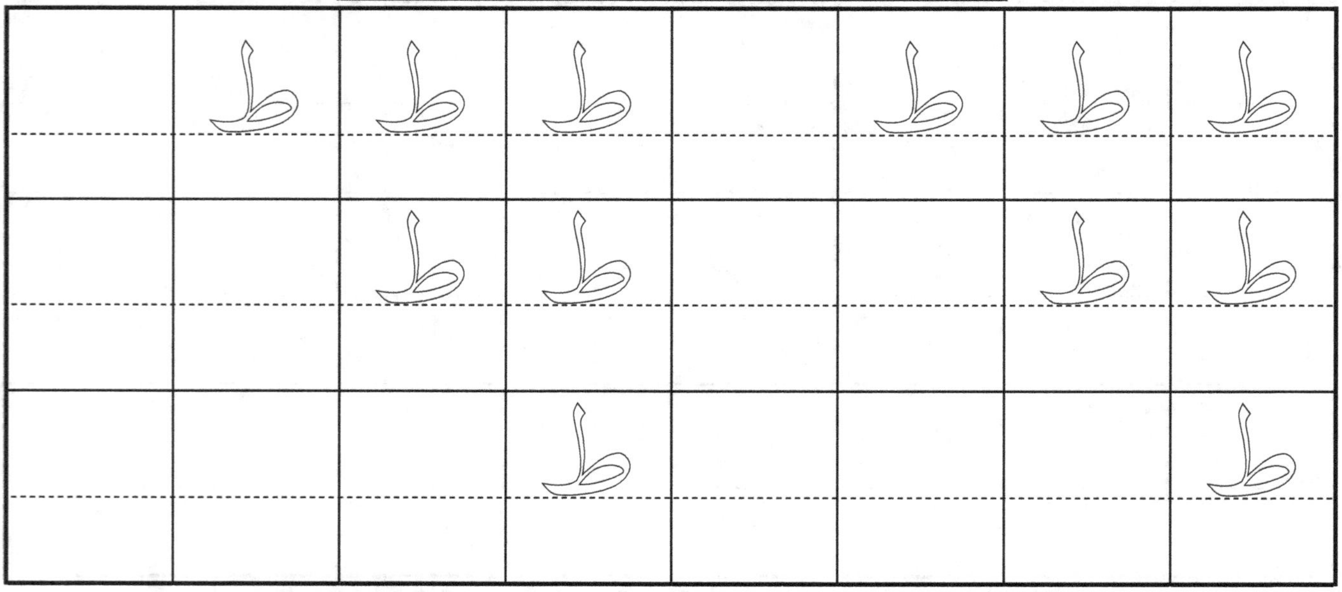

Common mistakes : *Drawing (3) too low to the base line.* ● *Not extending the tail long enough.* [Note : Incorrect]

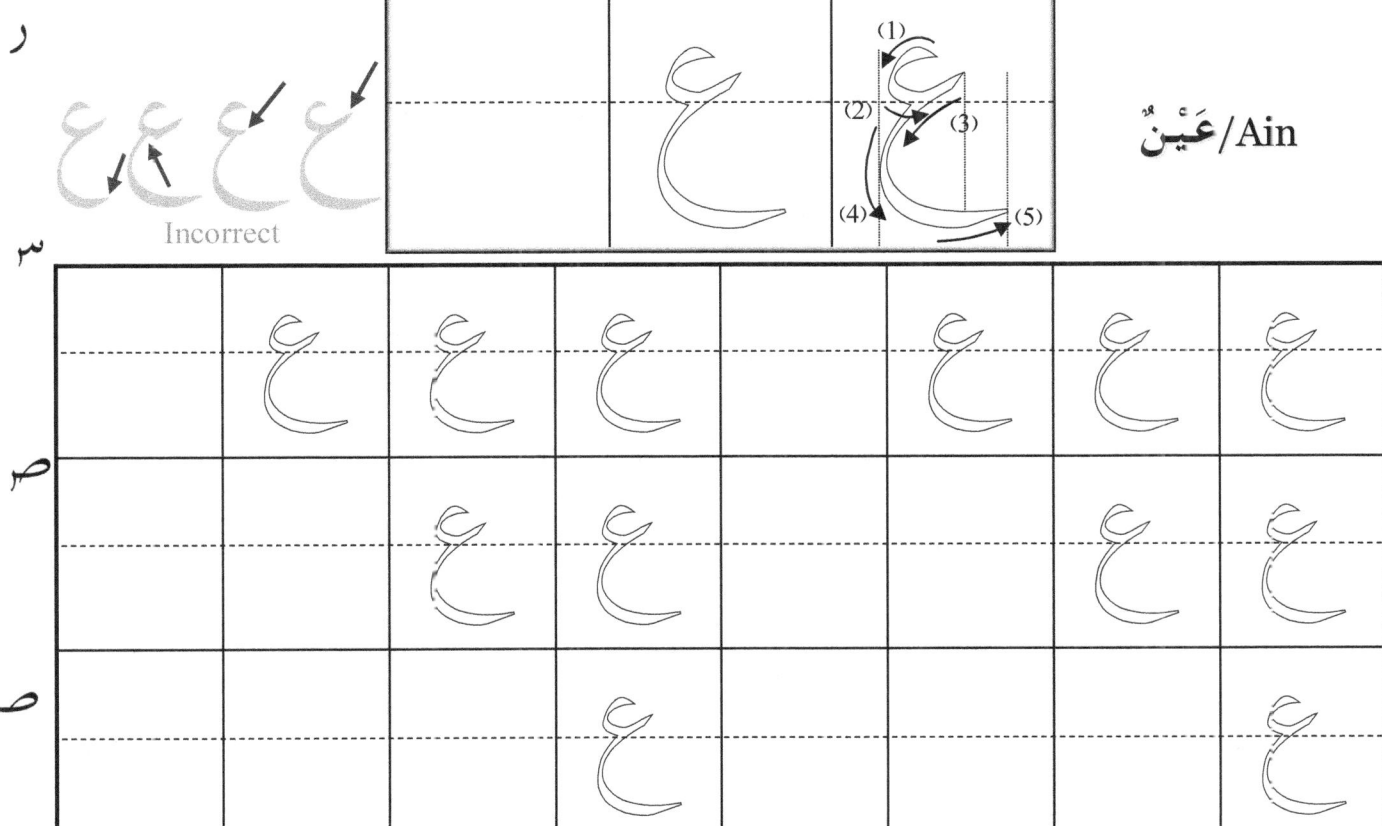

ظاء/Thaa أُ

ا

ٮ

ح

د

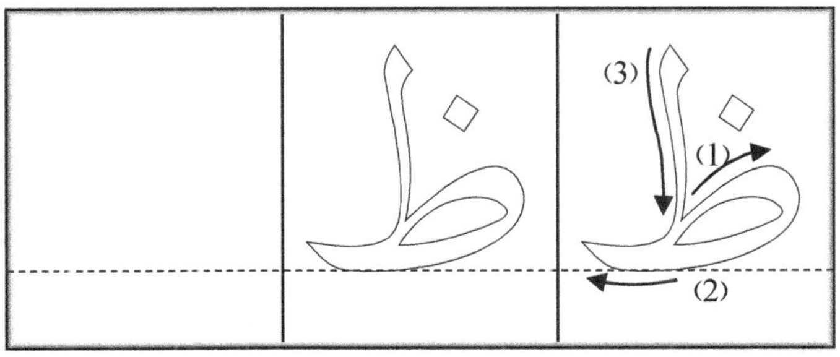

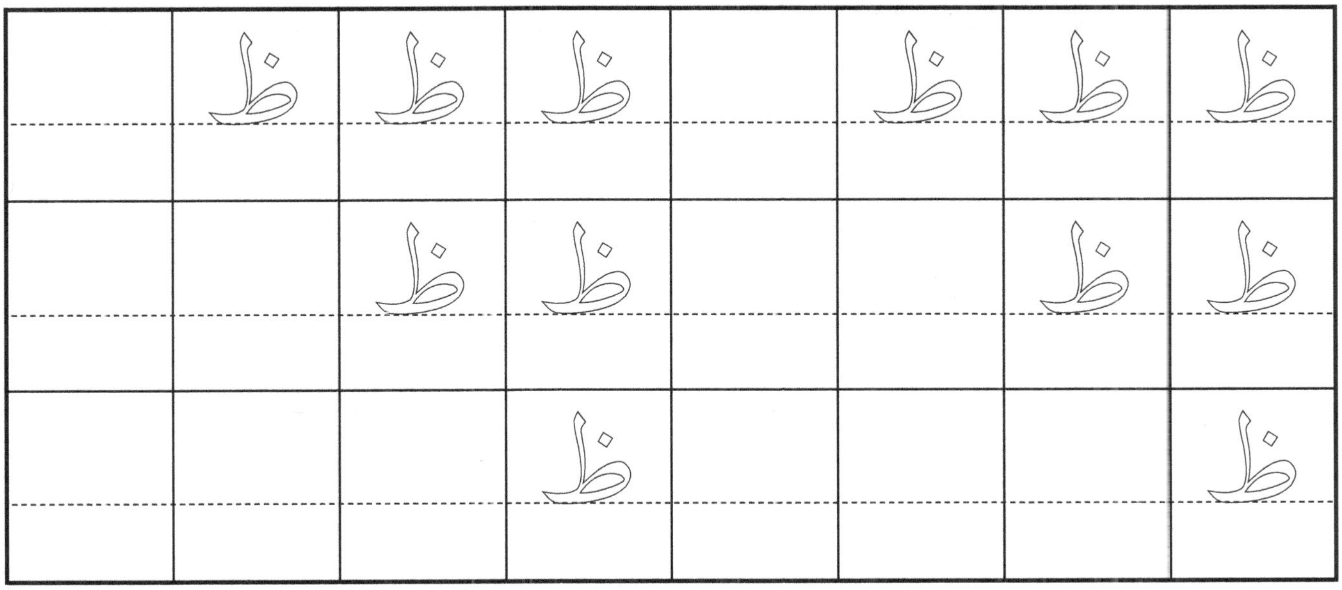

Common mistakes : Same as in the letter ط.

عَيْنٌ/Ain ر

Incorrect

٣

ع

٩

Common mistakes : Not curving (1) at the very beginning. ● Not extending (3) enough. ● Not extending (5) enough.

ع

21

٩

غَيْنٌ/Ghain

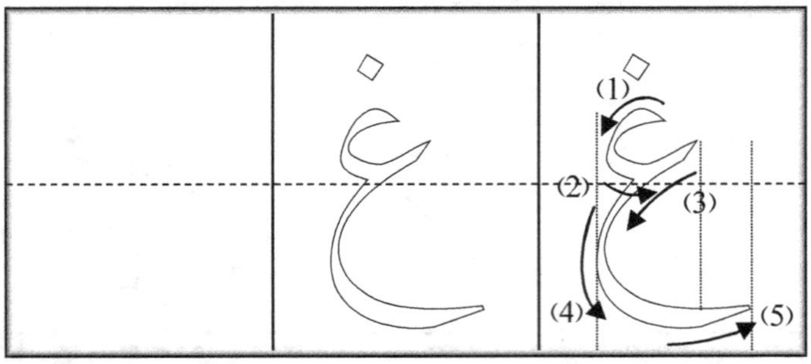

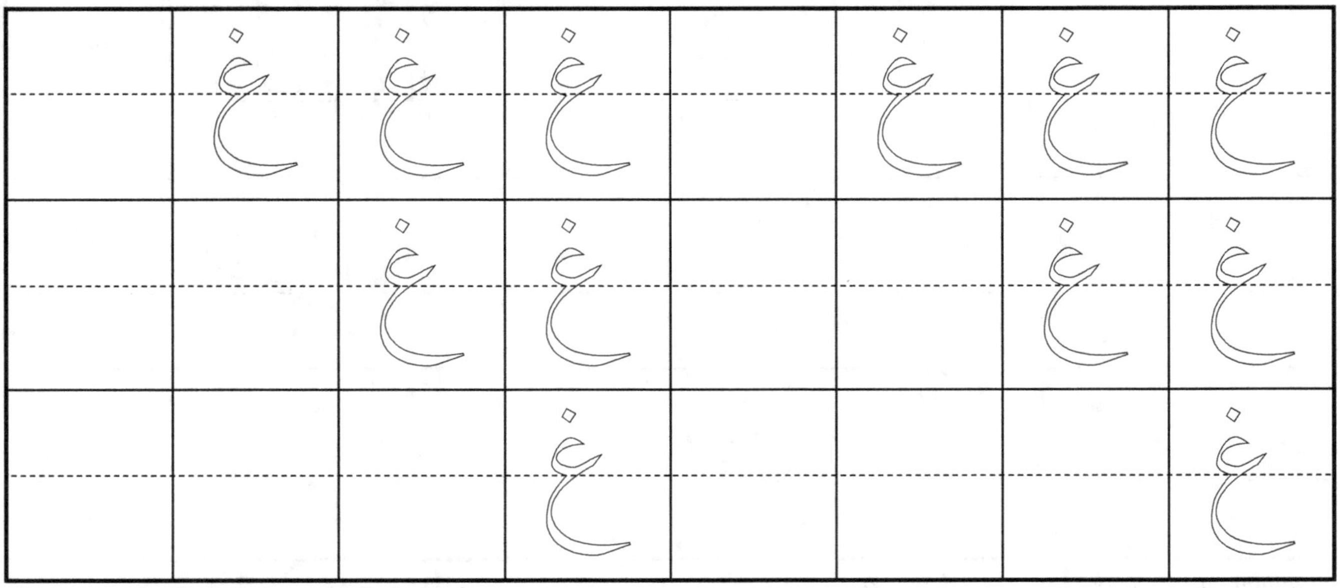

٩

د

ا

Common mistakes : Same as in the letter ع.

فاءٌ/Faa

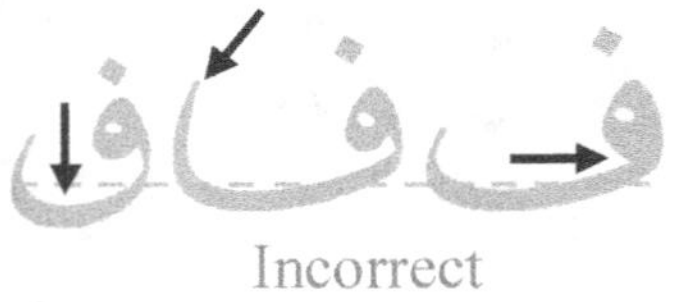

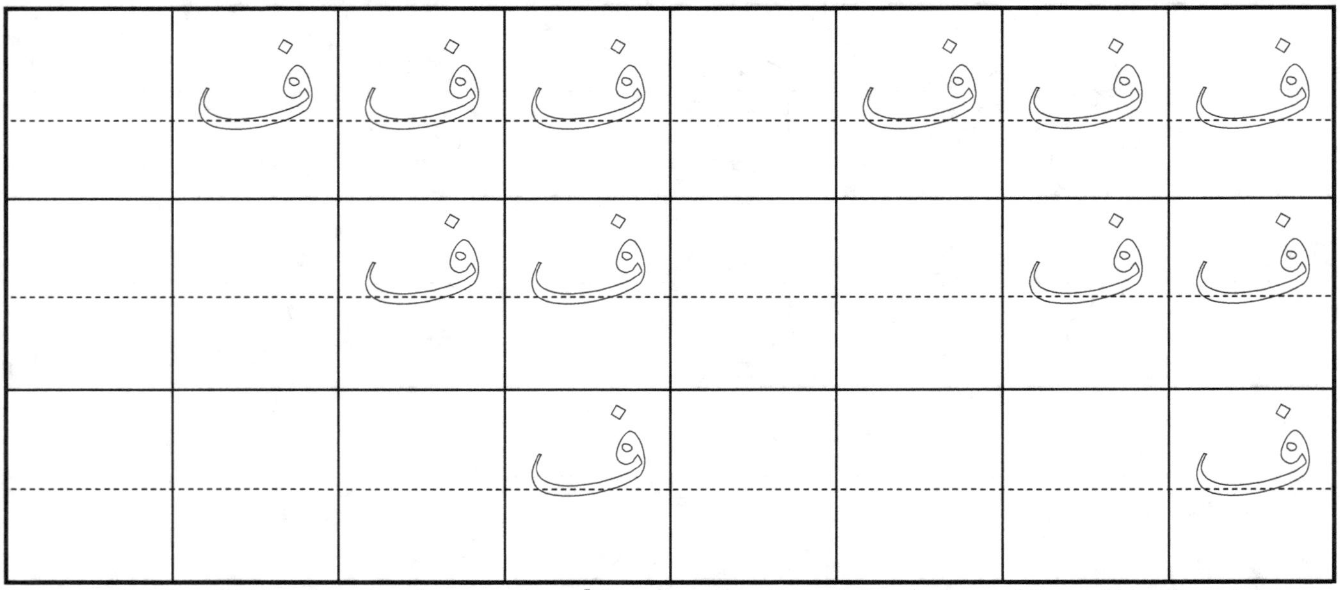

Incorrect

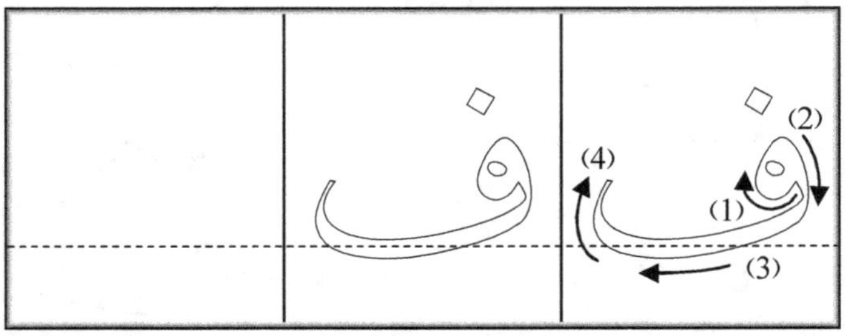

ر

د

ه

Common mistakes : Not leaving space between (١) and (٣). ● Drawing (٣) far below the ground line. ● Extending (٤) too high. [Note : Incorrect]

ي

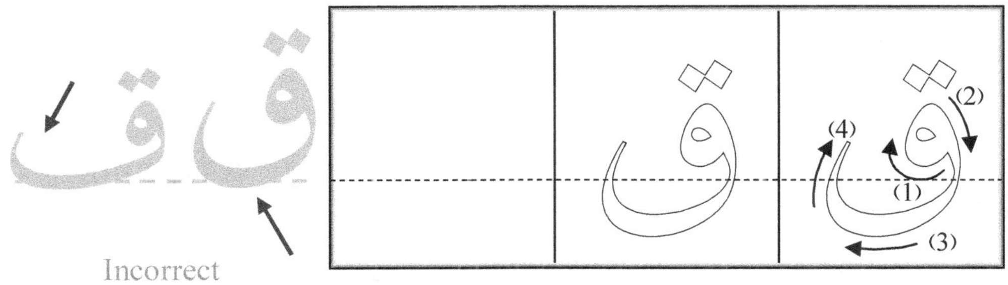

قـ قـ قـ

Incorrect

قِيافٌ/Qaaf ❀

| | | ق | ق |

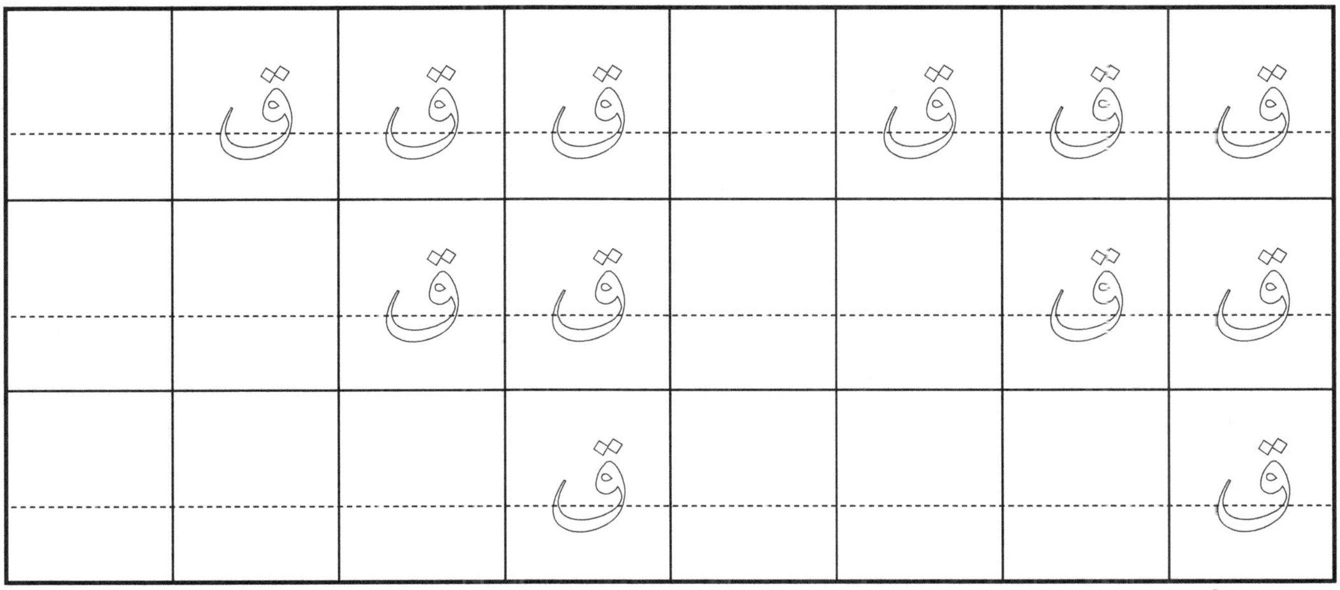

Common mistakes : *Not drawing (3) below the baseline.* ● *Extending (3), and therefore making it appear like* ف.

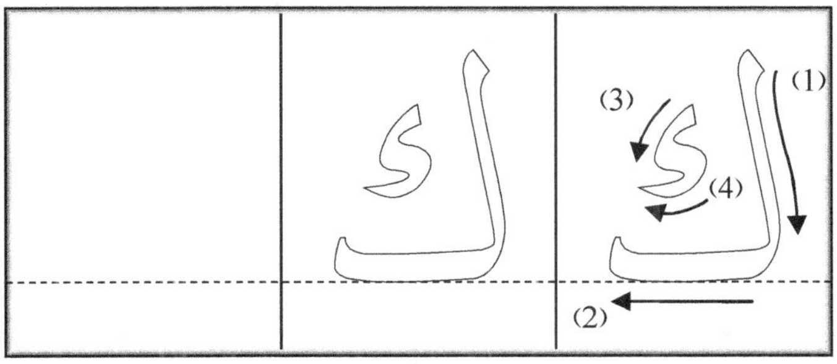

كَافٌ/Kaaf *❀

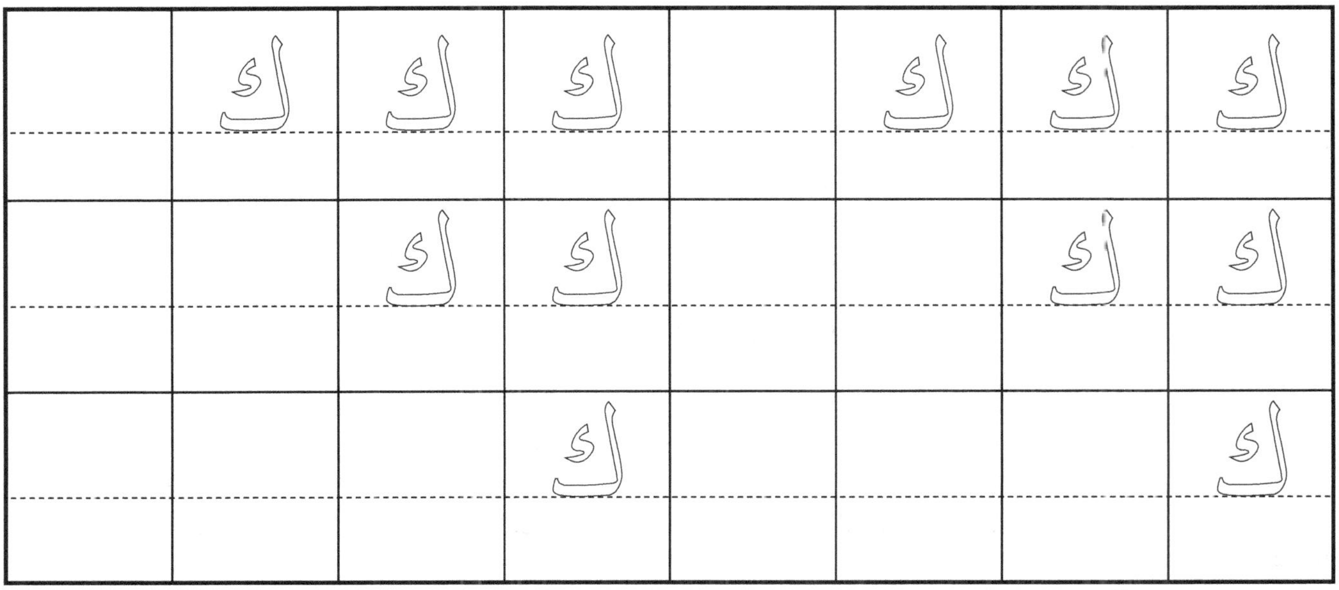

| | | ك | لَـ |

23 *Please note that this mark inside the letter is *not* the same as hamza as you can see here [كء ❀].

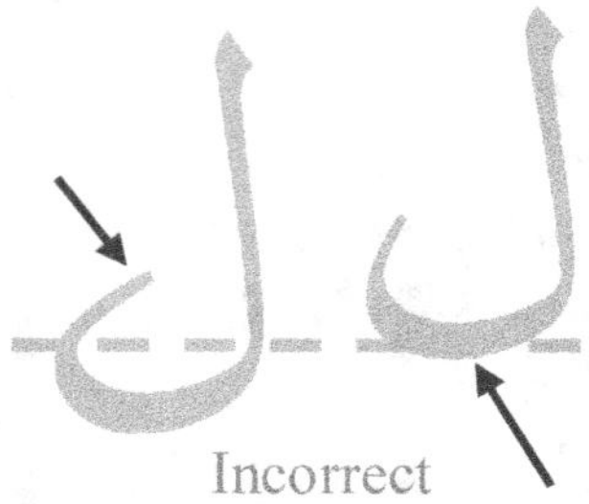

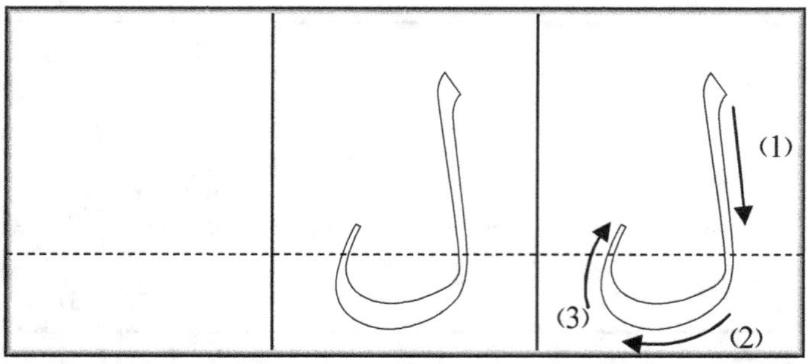

لاٌم/Laam

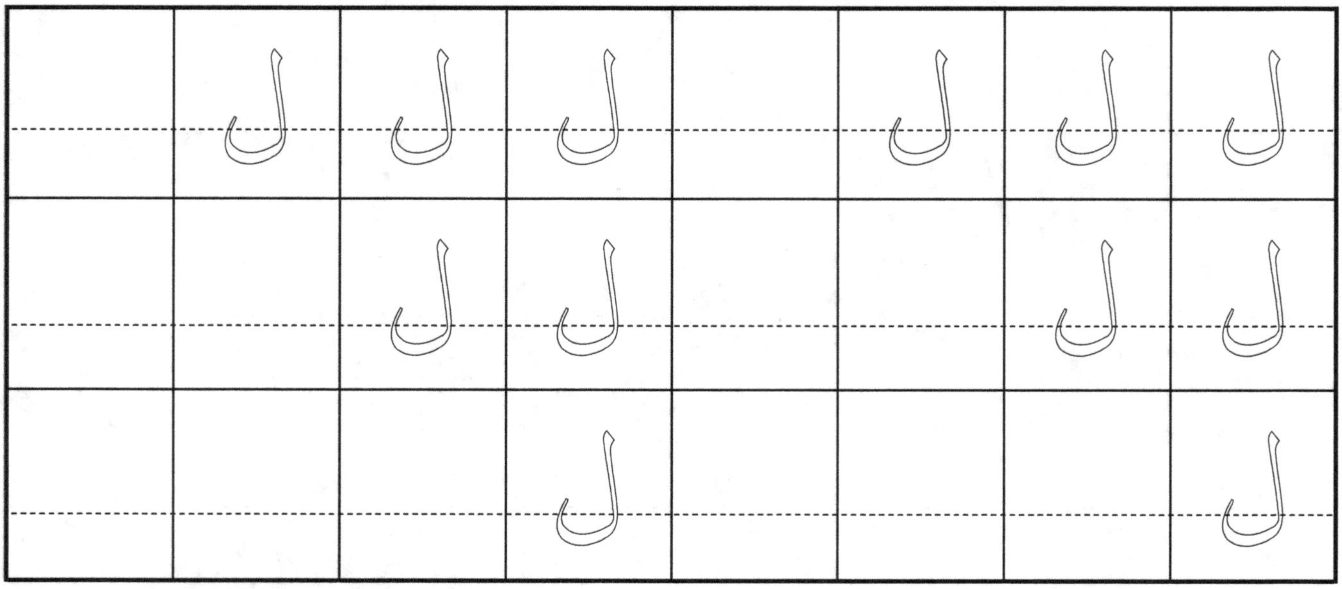

Common mistakes : *Not drawing (2) below the ground line, or, not enough below.* ● *Extending (3) too far to the right.*

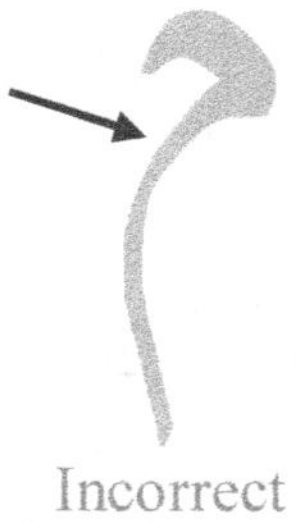

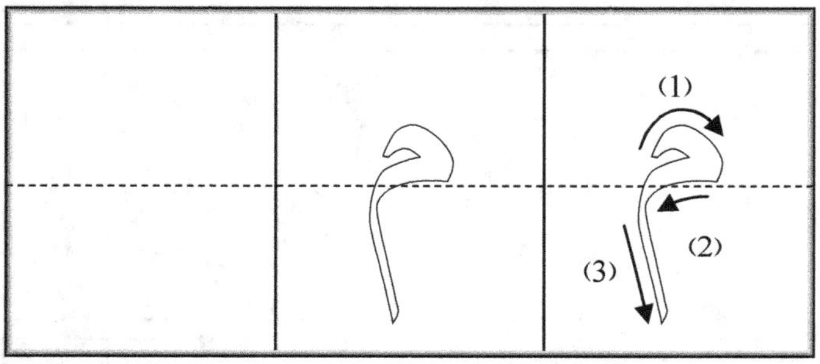

مِيْم/Meem

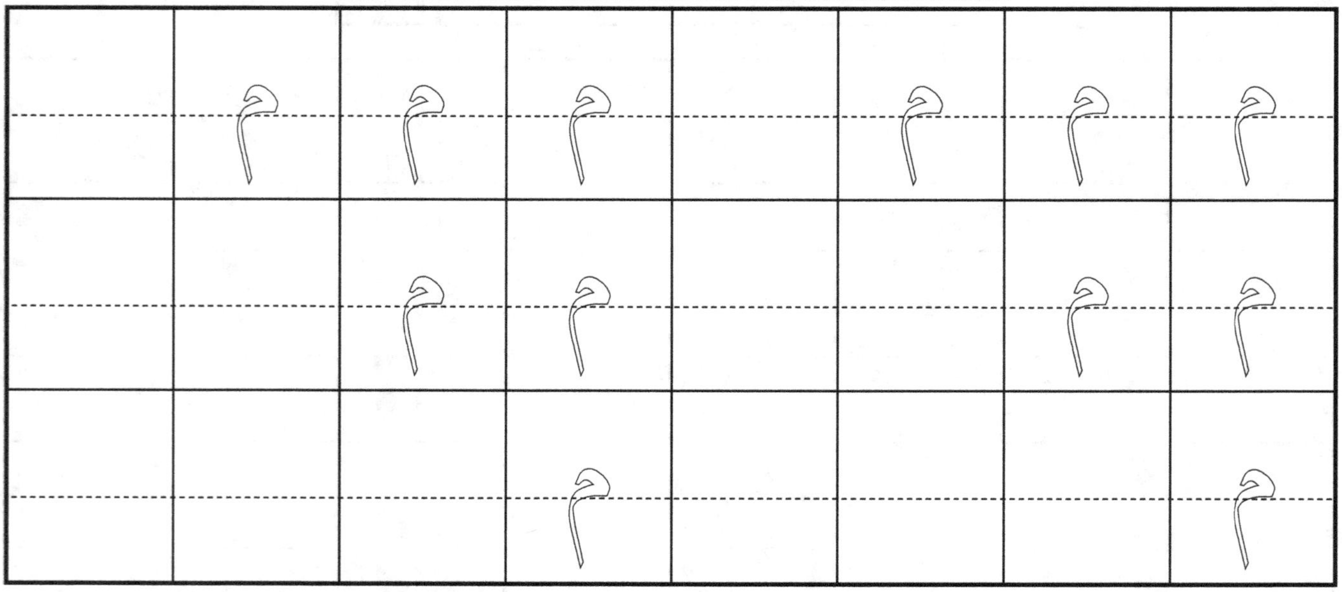

Common mistake : *Not drawing (2) enough to the left before continuing to (3).* [Note : Incorrect]

و

ل

د

ى

نُونْ/Nuun

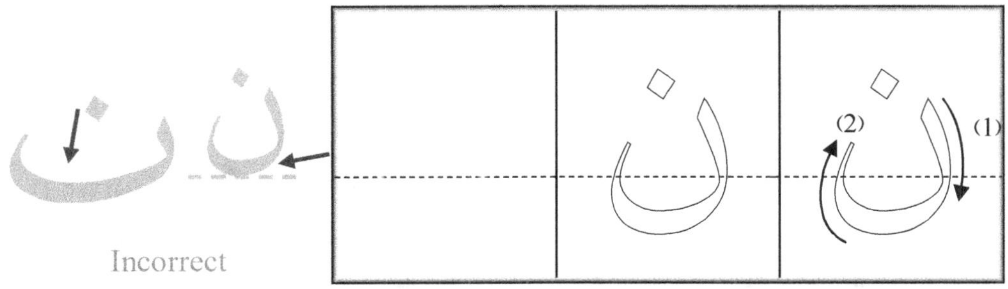

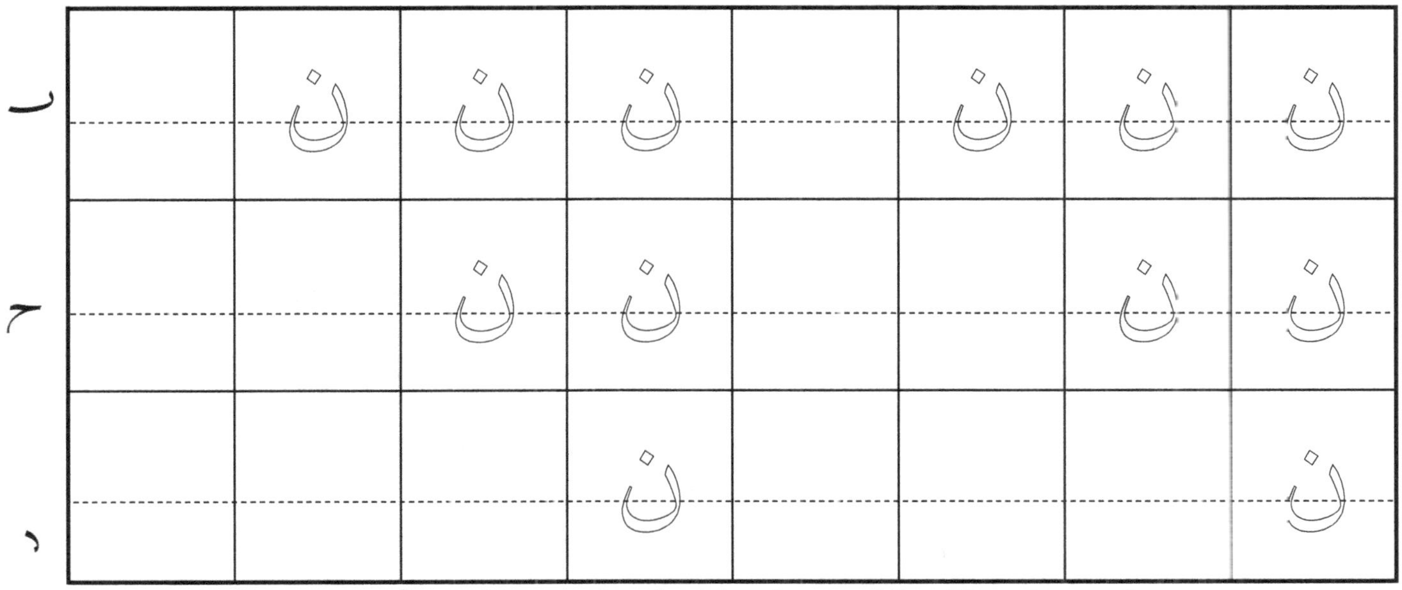

ن ن ن ← Incorrect

Common mistakes : Drawing ن too wide. ● Not drawing below the ground line. [Note : Incorrect]

هاء/Haa

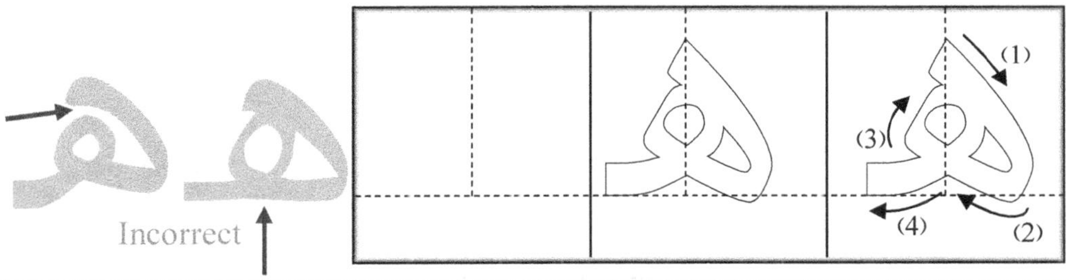

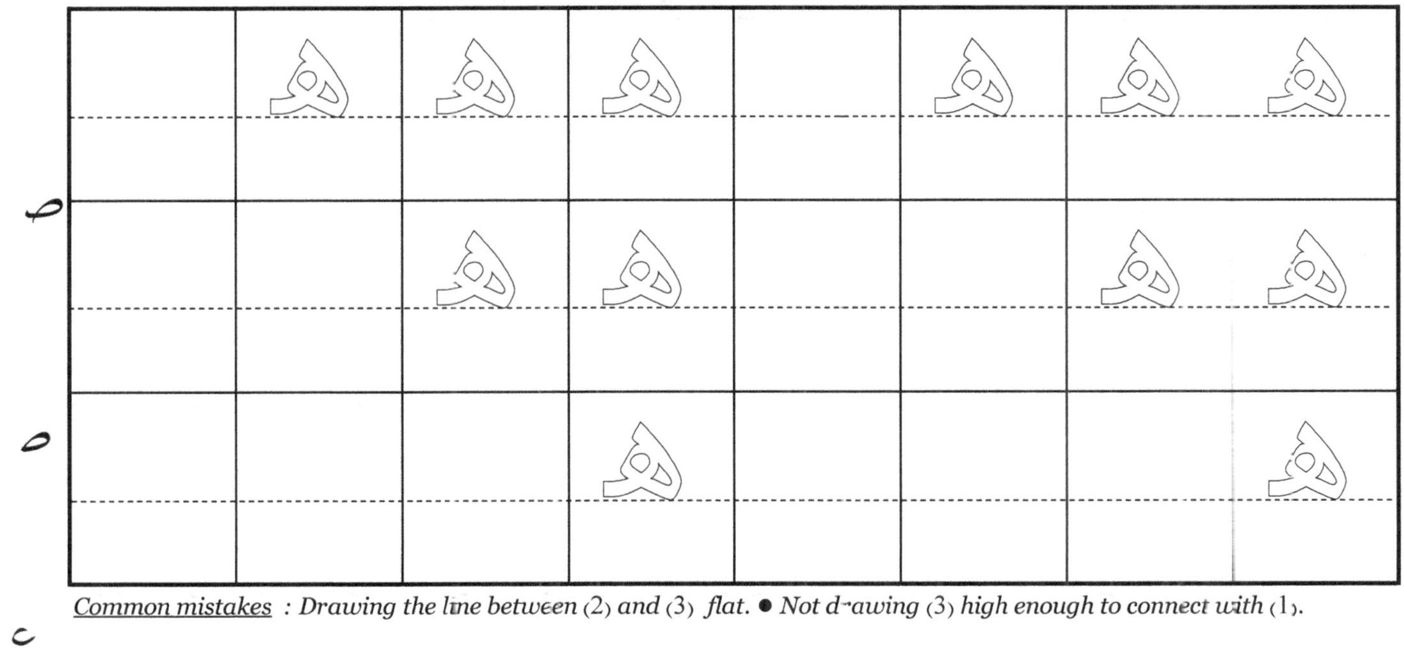

هـ هـ ← Incorrect

Common mistakes : Drawing the line between (2) and (3) flat. ● Not drawing (3) high enough to connect with (1).

ا
ب
ت
ث
ج
ح
خ

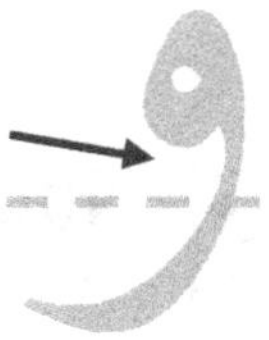

و ‏وَاوٌ/Waaw

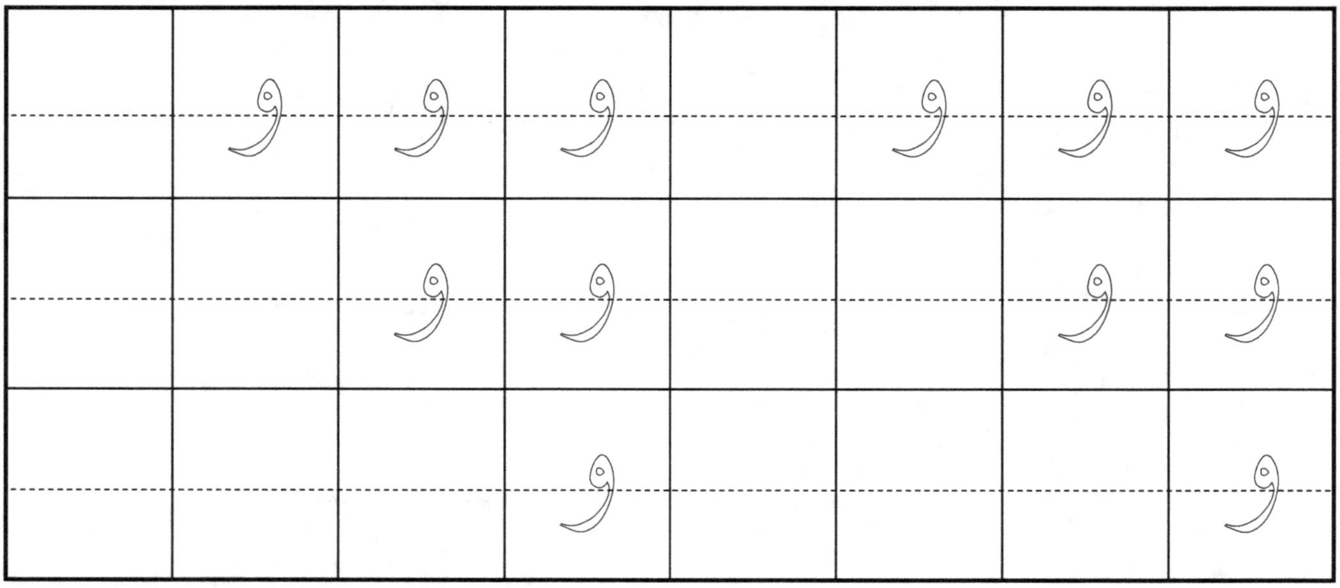

Incorrect

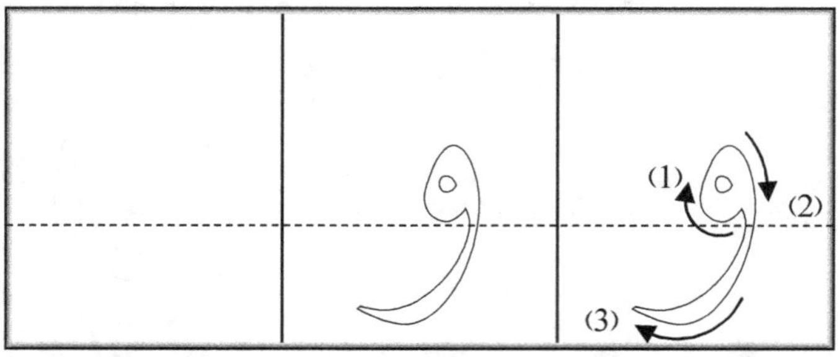

Common mistake : *Drawing the letter too high above the ground line.* [Note : Incorrect]

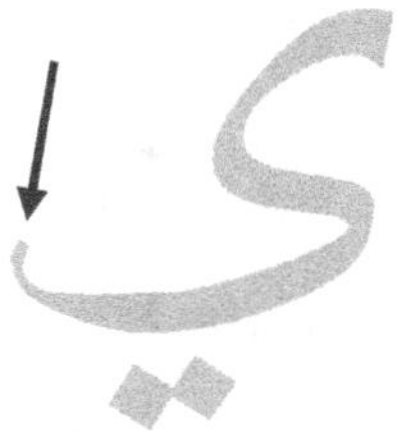

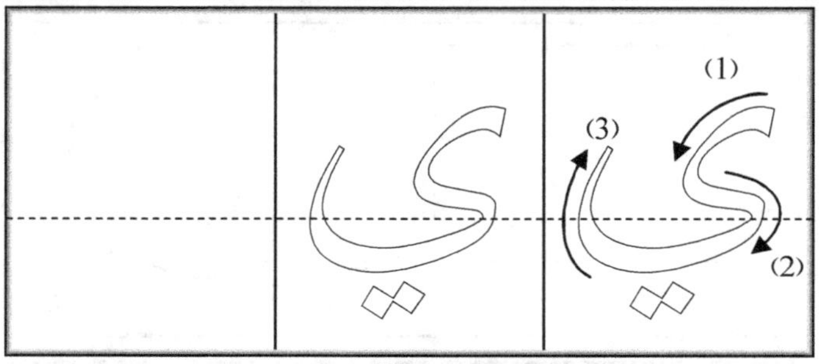

م

‏يَاءٌ/Yaa

ل

Incorrect

ه

و

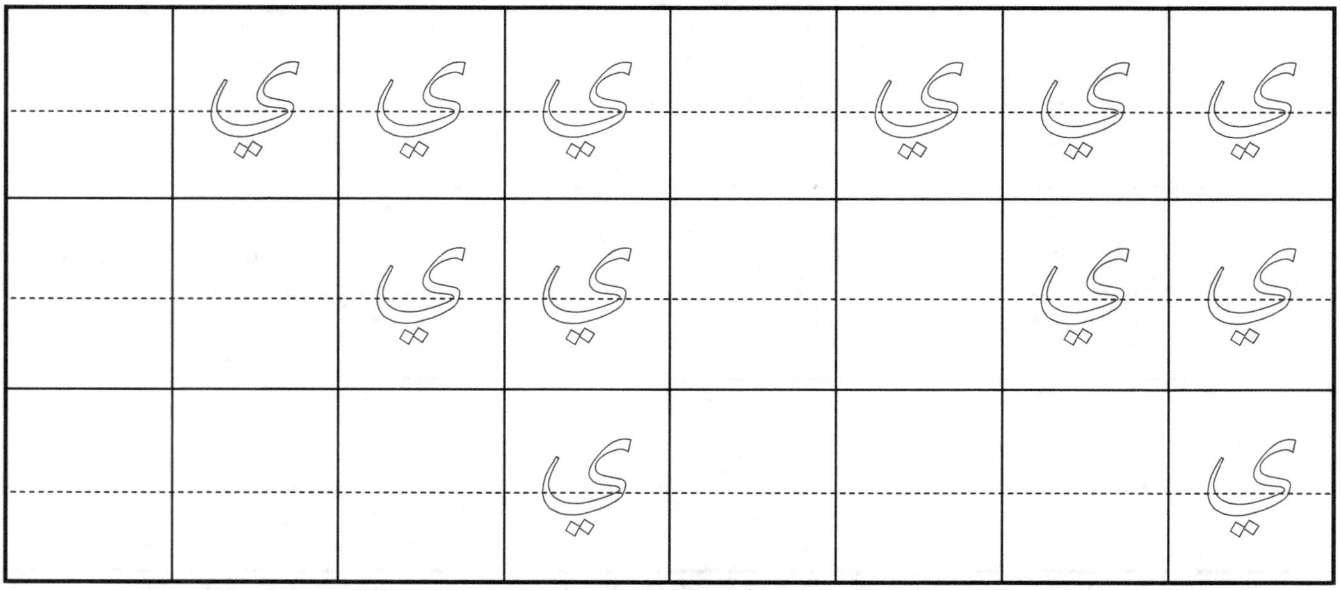

Common mistake : *Not drawing (3) high enough above the ground line.* [Note : Incorrect]

ى

و

ل

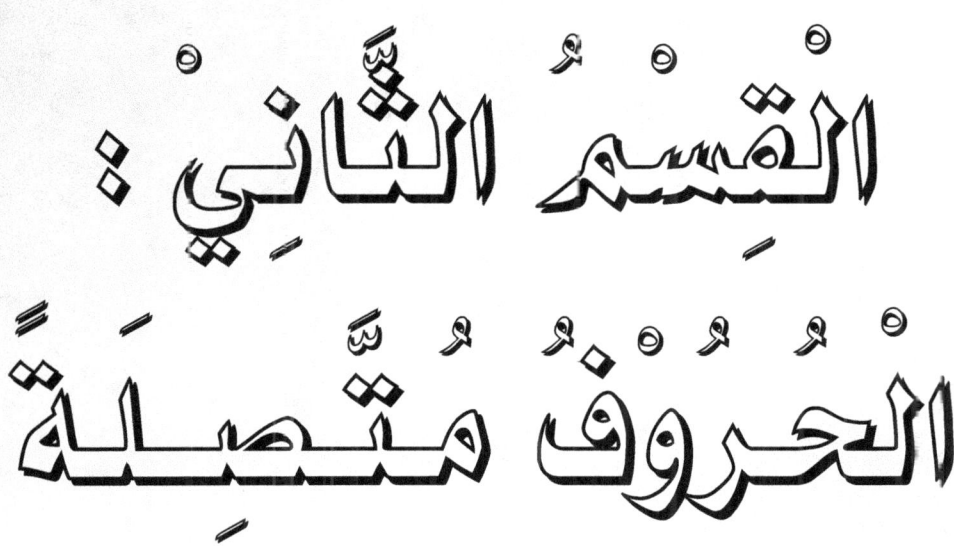

القِسْمُ الثَّانِي :

الحُرُوْفُ مُتَّصِلَةً

Part Two :

The Letters in Their Connected Forms

Letters have different forms depending on their position : isolated (as in the previous section), initial (at the beginning of a word), medial, and final.

In this section you will learn to write the initial, medial, and final forms.

Many of the combinations in this section have meanings in Arabic.

		باب	باب			باب باب	باب
		تاب			ذاب ذاب		ذاب
		باع					بات

		تيا	تيا			تيا تيا	تيا
		تبن			تبر تبر		تبر
		أبت					تاب

		ثيث	ثيث			ثيا ثيا	ثيا
		ثيا			يثث يثث		بثث
		باب					بثث

ف			بَجَرَ	بَجَرَ			بَجَرَ	بَجَرَ
ف			نَخَرَ	نَخَرَ			نَحَرَ	نَحَرَ
ئـ			جَا	جَا			جَا	بِجَا
ل			خَبِثَ	خَبِثَا			خِبِثَ	خِبِثَ
			يَجِيثَ					أُجِيثَ

بَـحَـر = بَحَر / تَـخَـم = تَخَم   م

ـ			بِيَخَل	بِيَخَل			يَبْحَر	يَبْحَر
هـ			خَالٌ	خَالٌ			حَالٌ	حَالٌ
و			يَخَل	يَخَل			يَحَر	يَحَر
			جِيب	جِيب			جِيب	جِيب
			أُجَاب				تَنْخَم	تَنْخَم
ى			تَخَم					تَنْجَم

30

د / ـد ✿ ذ / ـذ ✿

			أُبِدا أُبِدا	أُبِدا			بابْ بابْ	بابْ
			ثذا	ثذا ثذا			تدرْث تدرْث	تدرْث
				جدد			جذب جذب	جذب
				جذب				جذب

ر / ـر ✿ ز / ـز ✿

			ثاز ثاز	ثاز			ترك ترك	ترك
			ورد ورد	ورد			ورد	ورد
			حجز حجز	حجز			جذور جذور	جذور
				أرز			أرز أرز	أرز
				بثر			بادو بادو	بادو
				بادور				بادور

سـ / ـسـ / ـس / س

ق

		بسبب	بسبب			ست	ست

ف

| | | ست | ست | | | ست | ست |

ك

| | | حس | | | | ثسا | ثسا |

ل

| | | جسد | | | | جسر | جسر |

| | | ثسا | | | | ثسا |

م

شـ / ـشـ / ـش / ش

ن

		ثشب	ثشب			ثشب	ثشب

ه

| | | ثشا | ثشا | | | ثشا | ثشا |

و

| | | دبش | | | | جشر | جشر |

| | | بشو | | | | بشو | بشو |

ي

| | | ثشب | | | | ثشب |

32

ص / صـا / ص   ضـا / ضـا / ض

١			تصر	تصر			صيد	صيد
			صيد	صيد			صيد	صيد
			رص	رص			بصر	بصر
			يبصر	يبصر			يبصر	يبصر
			حض	حض			ضب	ضب
				ضب			ضب	ضب
				رضا			حضر	حضر
				غض				غض

ط / طـ   ظ / ظـ

			ظرف	ظرف			طفل	طفل
				نظر			لطف	لطف
				خطأ			نظر

		عاب	عاب			عاب	عاب
		عفا	عفا			عفا	عفا
		مع	مع			بعل	بعل
		بعل	بعل			بعل	بعل
		رغد	رغد			غدا	غدا
			غدا			غدا	غدا
			بلغ			بغد	بغد
			بغد				بغد

ف
ك
ل
م
ن

ه

ف

		فأر	فأر			فاز	فاز
			فاز				فاز

و
ي

34

ف / ـف / ـفـ

		خفّف	خفّف			حفظ	حفظ
			دفّ				لفّ

ق / ـق / ـقـ

		قبض	قبض			قط	قط
		رقص	رقص			فقد	فقد
			لحق			لقط	لقط
			ذاق				لحق

ك / ـك / ـكـ

		حكا	حكا			كتب	كتب
			فلك				كعب

35

فعل فعل

Incorrect / Correct

ف

		فعل	فعل			قلب	قلب
		لعب					لعب

ق

م / ـمـ / ـم

ك

م

Incorrect / Correct

ل

		ملأٌ	ملأٌ			مال	مال
		علم	علم			بكم	بكم
		بكم				لمس	لمس
		جمل				لمم	لمم

م

ن

ه

ن

		نبأٌ	نبأٌ			نبي	نبي
		أنت					نبأٌ

و

ي

36

		لجن	لجن	لجن		عنب	عنب
			كنس				خان

ه / ـهـ / ـه / ة

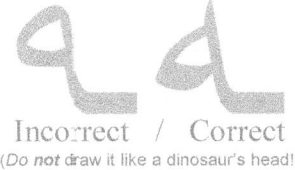

هـه
Incorrect / Correct
(*Do not* draw it like a dinosaur's head!)

		هرة	هرة	هرة		هبط	هبط
		لهب	لهب	لهب		لهث	لهث
			مياه			له	له
			هذا				لها

و / ـو

وو
Incorrect / Correct

		فوه	فوه	فوه		لغو	لغو
			خوف				واق

ي / ـي / اي / ـني

		ليـس	ليـس	ليـس		يقـن	يقـن
		بيـتي	بيـتي			لي	لي
			علـي			ليـت	ليـت
			نبـي				فـي

ف **ق** **ك**

ل

أ / إ / ئـ / ـئـ / ؤ / ـأ / ء / ئ

		إبـل	إبـل			أكل	أكل
		سائـر	سائـر			سئـل	سئـل
		ماؤه	ماؤه			ماؤه	ماؤه
		خطأ	خطأ			مؤمن	مؤمن
		خطأ					ملأ
		بارئ					ماء

م **ن** **ه** **و** **ي**

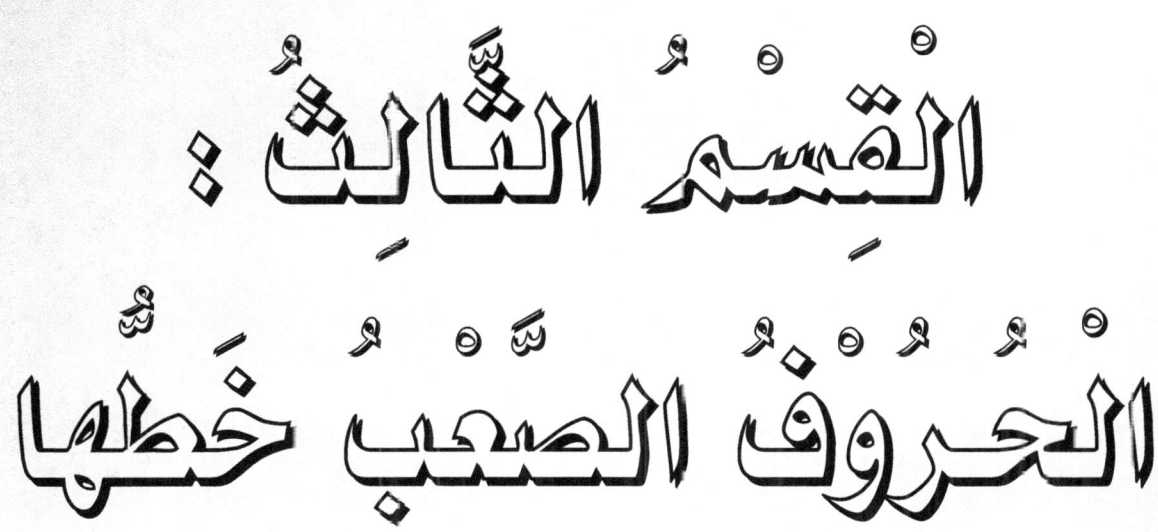

القِسْمُ الثَّالِثُ :
الْحُرُوفُ الصَّعْبُ خَطُّهَا

Part Three :

Difficult Letters

ف

ق

ك

ل

م

ن

ه

و

ي

40

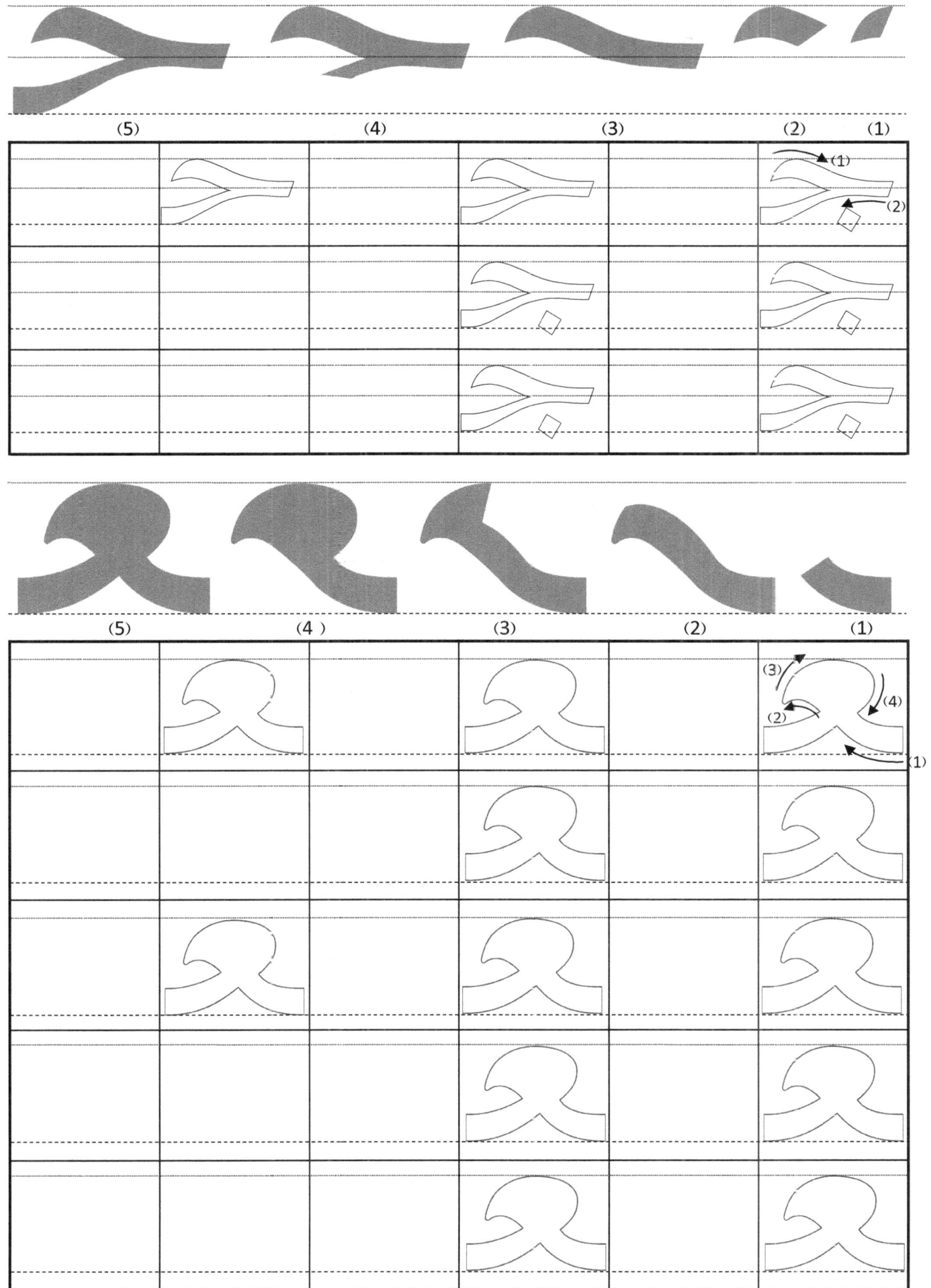

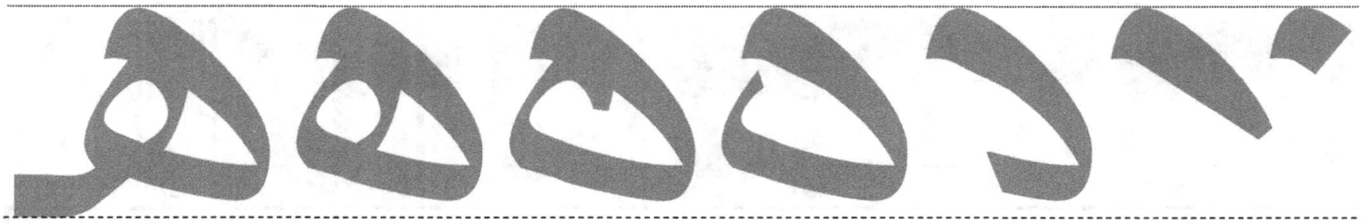

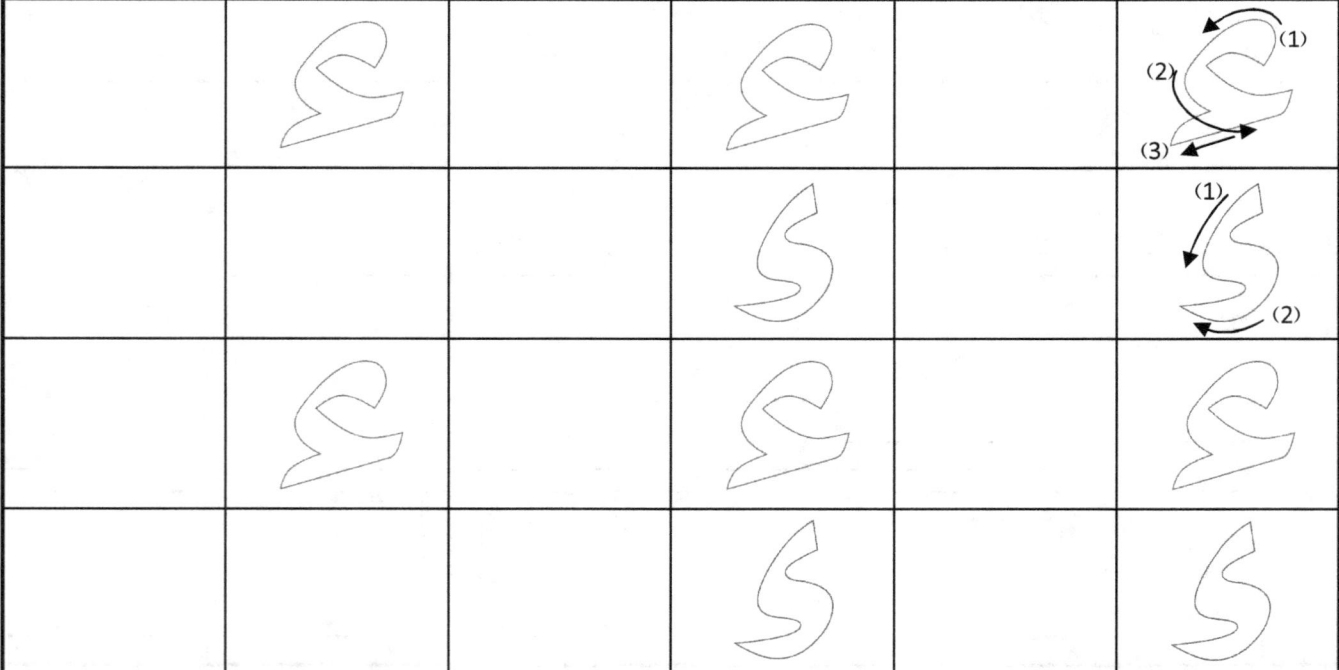

The hamza ع differs from the inside mark of the kaaf كـ.

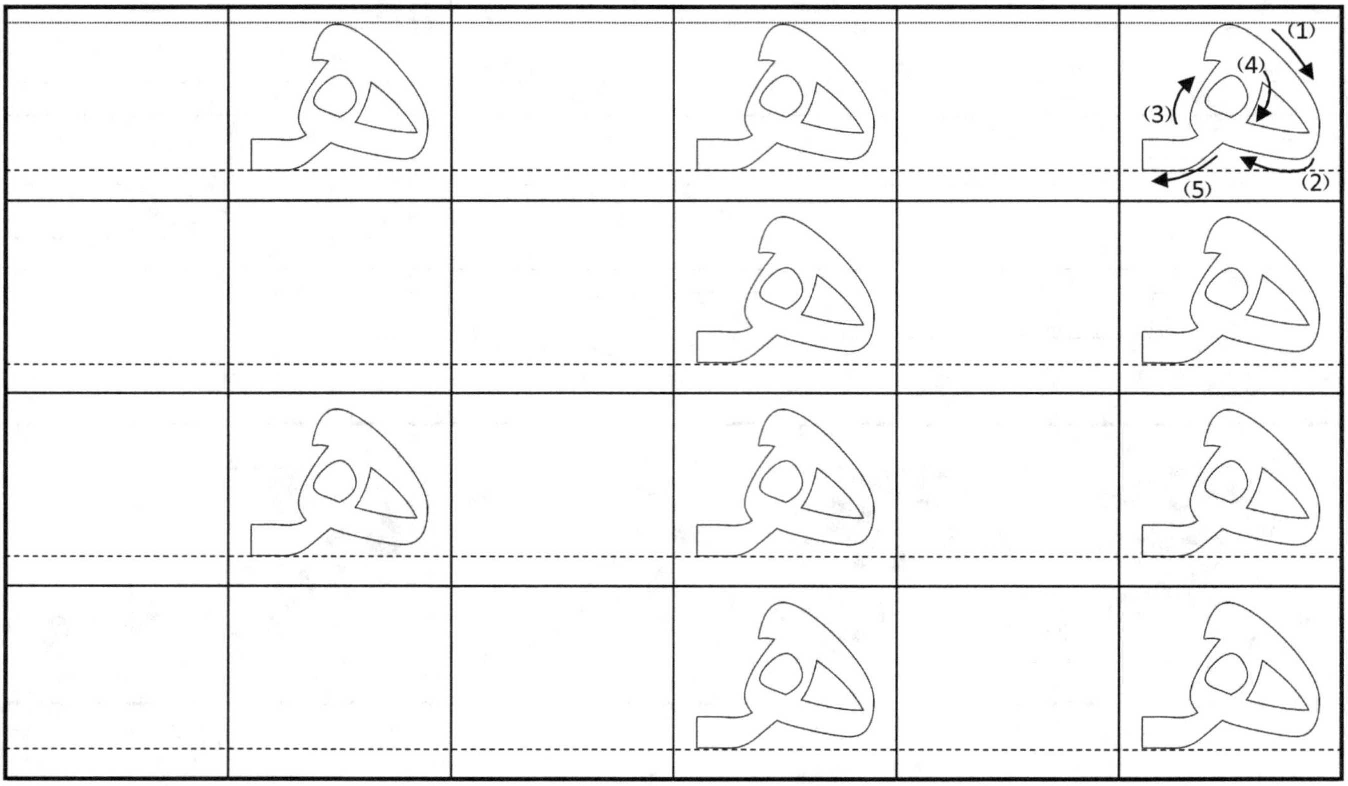

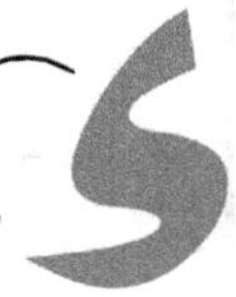

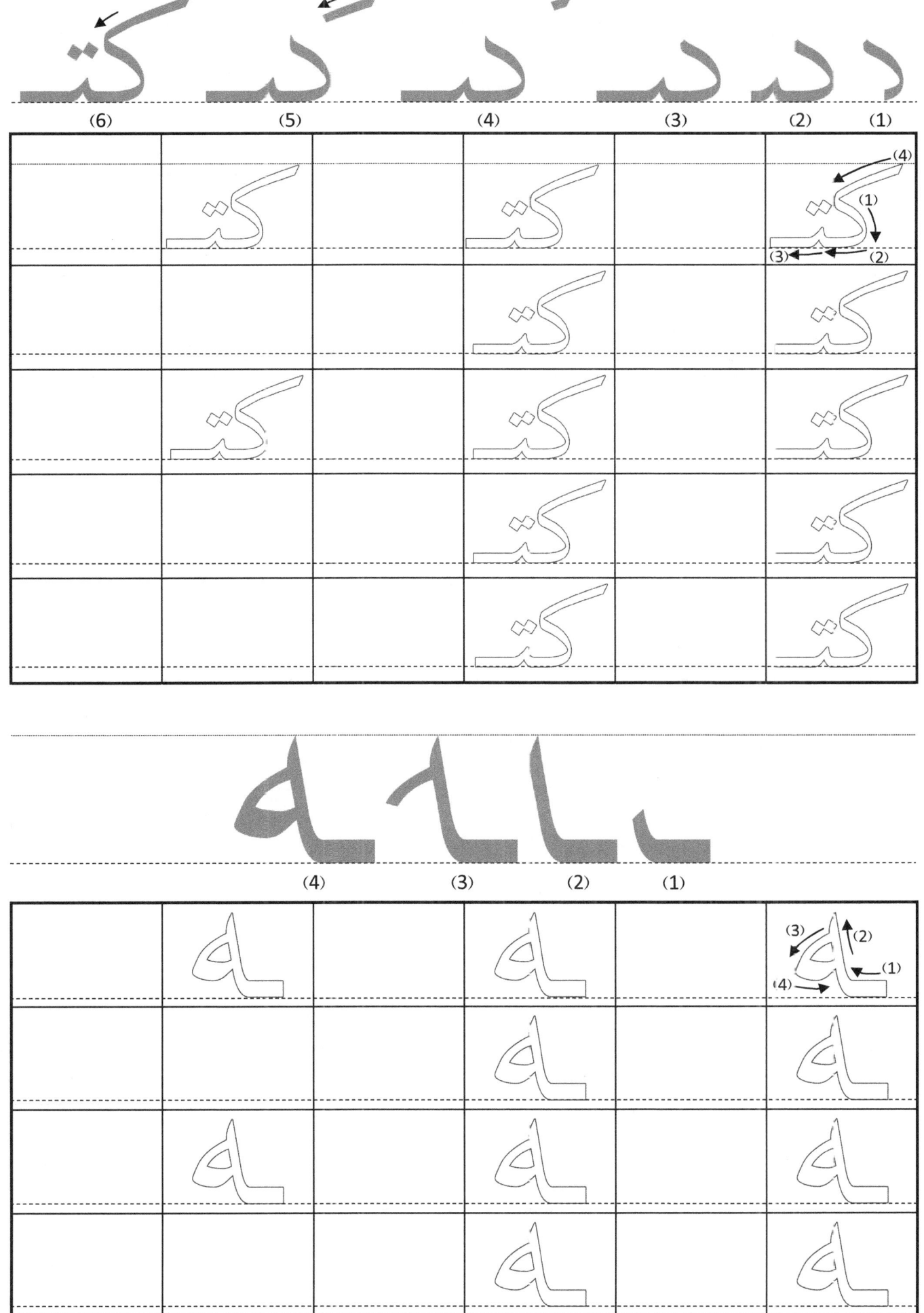

43

Note the difference between these two letters. 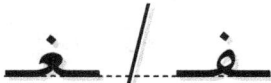 ـغـ / ـفـ

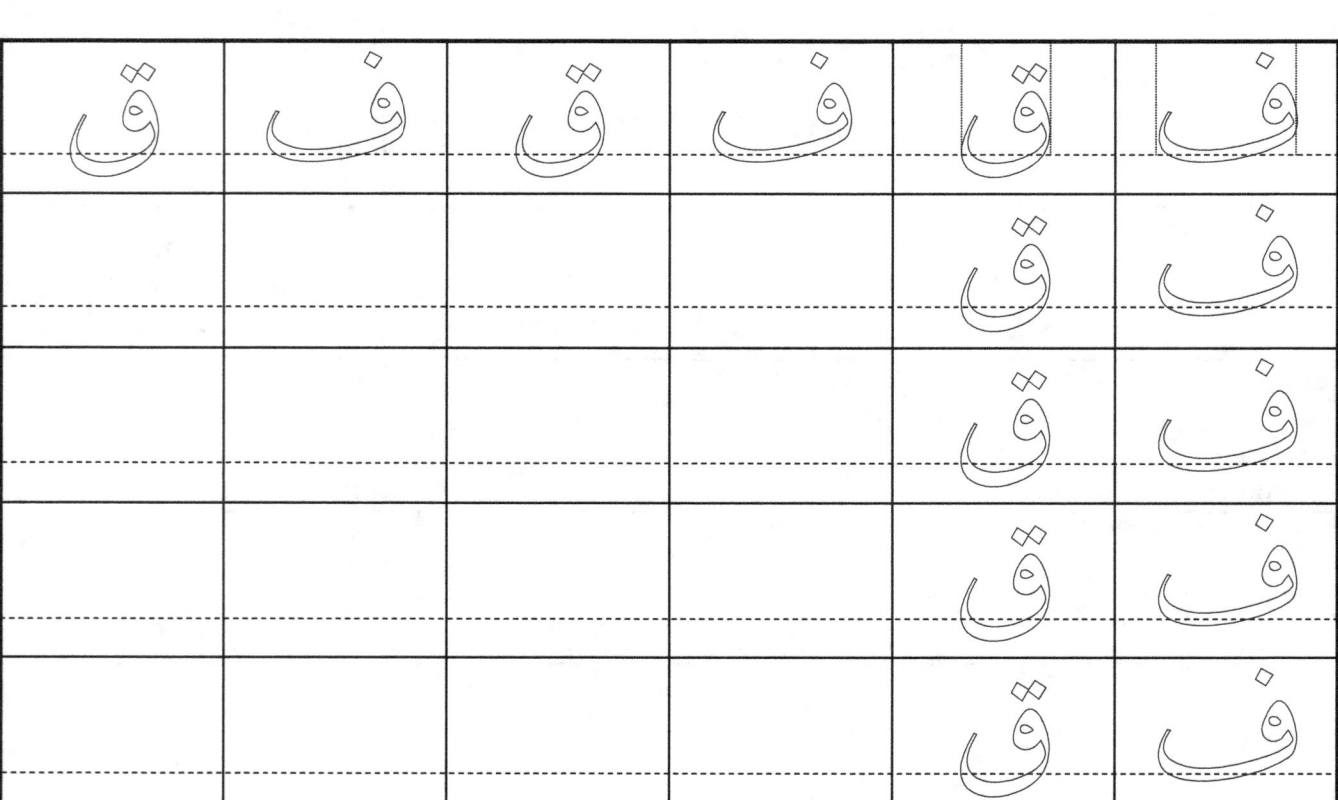

Note the difference between these two letters. ق / ف

Note the difference between these letters. دذ / رز

ز	ذ	ر	د	ر	د
				ر	د
				ز	ذ
				ر	د
				ز	ذ
				ر	د

The words of the first children's book

هذا هذ' هذ هد ه ه ه ١

	هذا	هذا		هذا	هذا

كتاب كتاب دتاب دماب دما دما د د ١

	كتاب	كتاب		كتاب	كتاب

نعم نعم نعم لعم لعم لع لع ل ١

	نعم	نعم		نعم	نعم

ـ د ـم ـمـ مـس مـسـ مـسـ مسحا مسحد مسجد

	مسجد مسجد	مسجد		مسجد مسجد

ه ه فا فا ـر فاس فاص فاص فاصه فاصة فاطمة فاطمة

	فاطمة فاطمة	فاطمة		فاطمة

ـ ع عا عاد عايد عايس عايسه عايشة عائشة عائشة

	عائشة عائشة	عائشة		عائشة

ـ ه ـم مـد مـد مـسـ مـسـ مـكتب مكتب مكتب

	مكتب مكتب	مكتب		مكتب مكتب

ا ا اال الد الد الحد الحد الدبر الدبير الكبير الكبير الكبير

	الكبير الكبير	الكبير		الكبير الكبير

ه و قص قص فض وط قط

	قط قط	قط		قط

ا ا اال الط الط الطء الطـ الطـ الطبة الطبية الطبيبة الطبيبة

	الطبيبة الطبيبة	الطبيبة		الطبيبة الطبيبة

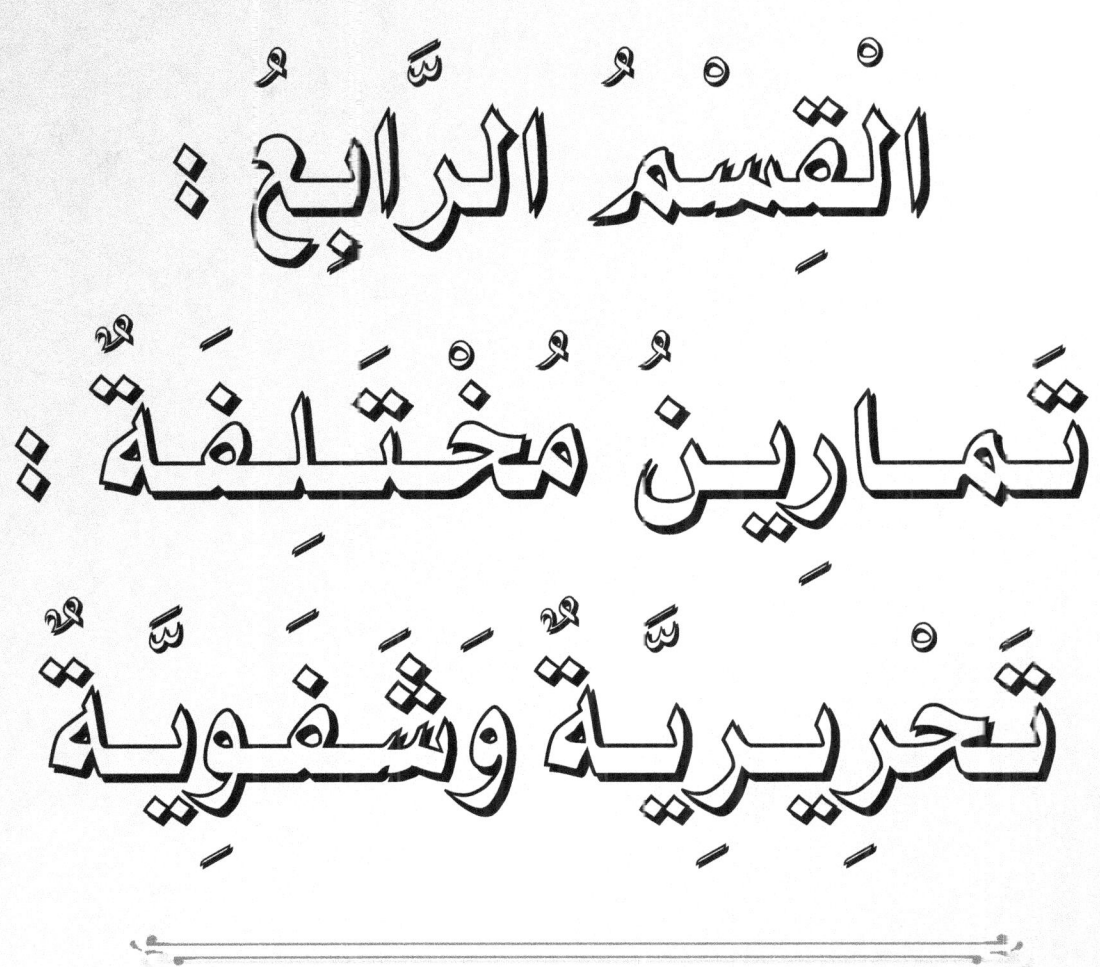

الْقِسْمُ الرَّابِعُ :
تَمَارِينُ مُخْتَلِفَةٌ :
تَحْرِيرِيَّةٌ وَشَفَوِيَّةٌ

Part Four :

Various Exercises : Written and Oral

The student is encouraged to write the following also :

   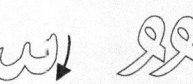 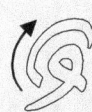

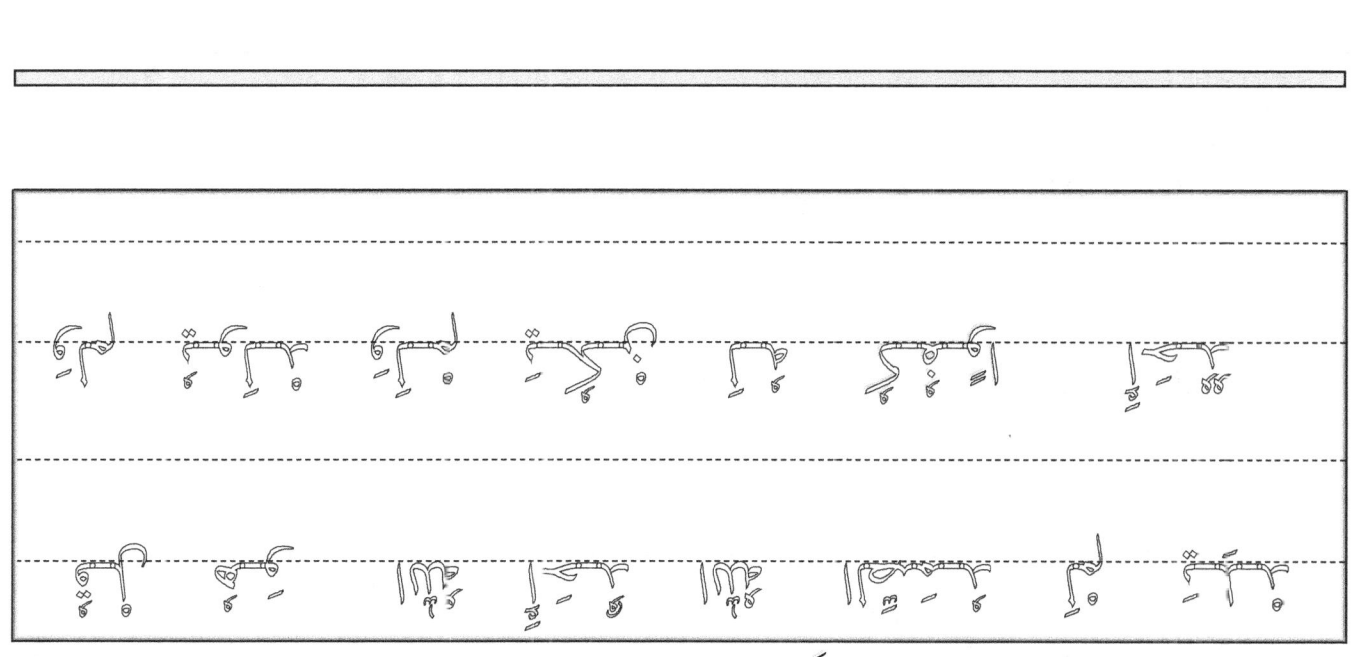

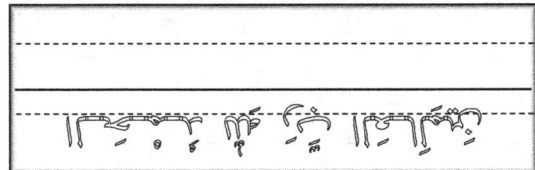

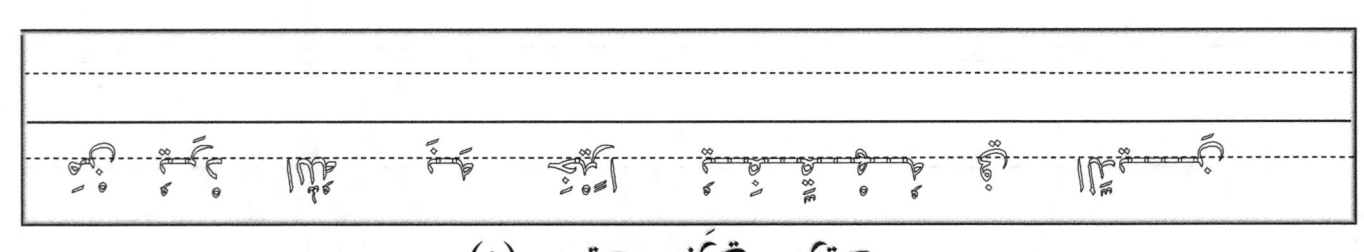

(2) الجملة اللحنية في المقام الرست

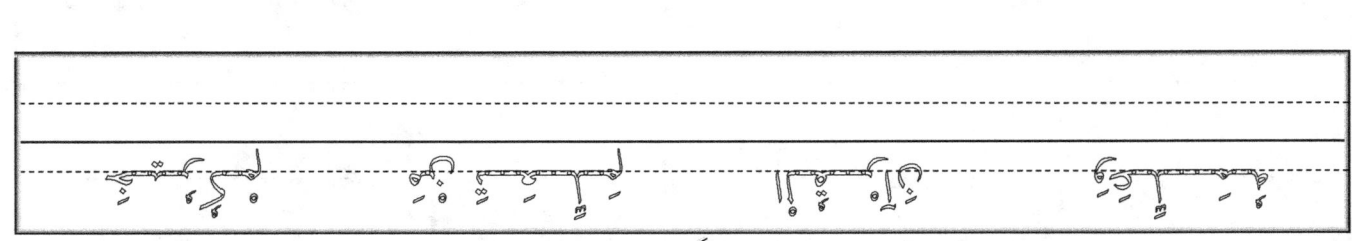

(1) الجملة اللحنية في المقام الرست

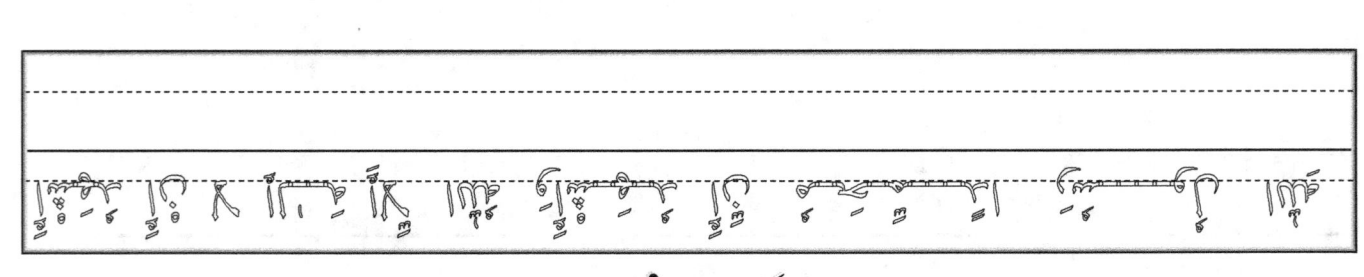

(1) Oral Exercise : Isolated Letters

Upon finishing the previous sections, the teacher should have the students write *letters* as they are read aloud.

(2) Oral Exercise : Connected Letters

Upon finishing (1) Oral Exercise, the teacher should have the students write the *letter combinations* as they are read aloud.

About The Author

Muhammad Taha Abdullah is an American convert to Islam since 1989. He studied at the Islamic University of Medinah, Saudi Arabia in the early 1990's. He is forty-four years old, married, has nine children and resides in Malaysia. He has been teaching Arabic for almost twenty years, and has written over 25 books related to Dr V. Abdur Rahim's revolutionary books and methodology.

About The Reviser

Dr V. Abdur Rahim is an outstanding Scholar of Arabic Language. He was Professor of Arabic for 30 years at the world renowned Islamic University, Medinah, Saudi Arabia, and has been teaching Arabic to non-native speakers for 50 years. He is currently the director of the Translation Centre at the King Fahd Qur'an Printing Complex.

How This Book Was Made

This book was created with Microsoft Word 2007, Adobe Illustrator and Photoshop (Middle Eastern versions) were used for the drawings, illustrations and pictures which were then inserted into Word. The Word document was converted into a PDF using Adobe Acrobat Pro version 9.0.

The most commonly used fonts are Tahoma, Trebuchet MS, and Georgia for English, and Traditional Arabic (خط عادي) and Uthman Taha Naskh (خط عثمان طه) for Arabic. I've modified the Traditional Arabic font using a font creator program. Font sizes range from 130 points to 18.

Please visit our websites :

www.DrVaniya.com   **www.Taha-Arabic.com**

Books By Muhammad Taha Abdullah and Dr V. Abdur Rahim :

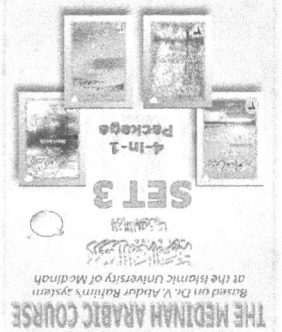
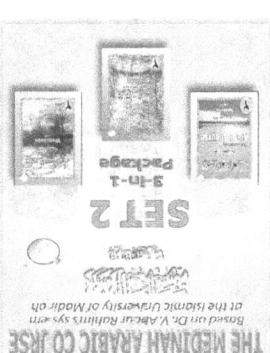
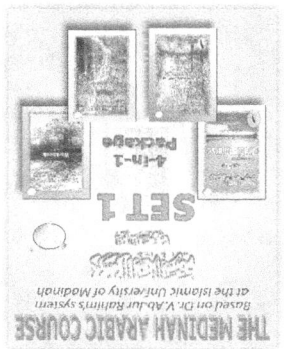
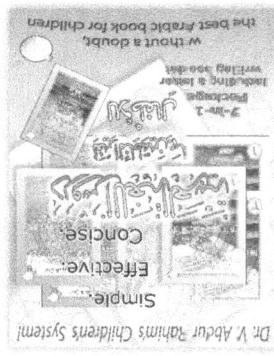

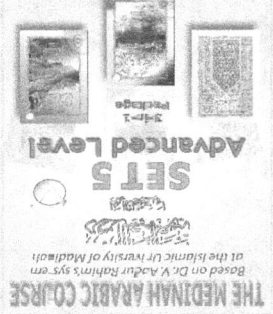
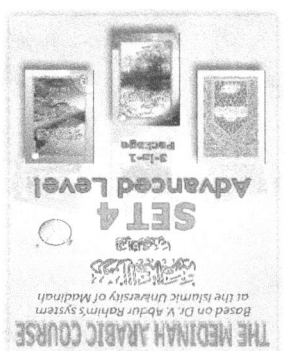
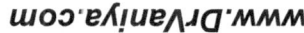